THE AGE OF SAIL

THE AGE OF SAIL

MASTER SHIPBUILDERS OF THE MARITIMES

STANLEY T. SPICER

FORMAC PUBLISHING COMPANY LIMITED
HALIFAX
2001

Illustration Credits and Sources

Abbreviations

AHPF: Alberton Historical Preservation Foundation; ARHSM: Avon River Heritage Society Museum; CCAGM: Confederation Centre Art Gallery & Museum; DUA: Dalhousie University Archives; FMA: Fisheries Museum of the Atlantic; MMA: Maritime Museum of the Atlantic; NAC: National Archives of Canada; NBM: New Brunswick Museum; NSARM: Nova Scotia Archives and Records Management; PANB: Provincial Archives of New Brunswick; PEIMHF: Prince Edward Island Museum and Heritage Foundation; PEIPARO: Prince Edward Island Public Archives and Records Office; YCM: Yarmouth County Museum

p. 1 MMA; p.3 MMA; p.8 YCM (Artist: Sarah Bond Farish); p.9 MMA (MP300.12.2; Neg 2722)

Chapter 1: p.12: NBM Artist: Sam Manning); p.13 PANB; p.14 NAC (PAC/AP C C-19294) (Artist: James Cummings Clarke); p.15 PANB; p.16 PANB Issac Erb Collection; p.17 NSARM (loc. 42.37 #1979-147.504) (Artist: William Bartlett); p18 PANB; p.19 PANB; p.20 PANB; p.22 PANB; p.23 R. Thresher, Courtesy of Parks Canada and the Province of New Brunswick; p.24 MMA (MP218.2.1); p.26 McCord Museum (Notman Archives; 1-76319); p.27 NAC (C17565)

Chapter 2: p.29 MMA; pp.30-31 PEIMHF (HF.74.12.4)(Artist: George Hubbard) p.32 PEIPARO (2670-28B); p.33 PEIPARO (2843-10); p.34 AHPF (986.12-306); p.35 McCord Museum (Notman Archives; 8287); p.36 bottom left, CCAGM (Gift of the Robert Harris Trust, 1965; CAGH-215)(Artist: Robert Harris); p.36 top, Meacham's Illustrated Historical Atlas of Prince Edward Island (1880); p.38 Meacham's Illustrated Historical Atlas of Prince Edward Island (1880); p.39 NAC (PA 122655); p.40 Nicolas J. de Jong and Marven E. Moore, Launched from Prince Edward Island (Prince Edward Island Heritage Foundation, 1981), p. 125; p.41 right, Photo, Patrick Chan; p.41 top, PEIPARO (2320-58-11); p.42 Mariners' Museum; p.43 Meacham's Illustrated Historical Atlas of Prince Edward Island (1880); p. 44 Nicolas J. de Jong and Marven E. Moore, Launched from Prince Edward Island (Prince Edward Island Heritage Foundation, 1981), p.126; p.45 PEIPARO (2301-51); p.45 Meacham's Illustrated Historical Atlas of Prince Edward Island (1880); p.47 Meacham's Illustrated Historical Atlas of Prince Edward Island (1880)

Chapter 3: p.49 NAC (Artist: John Hamilton); p.50 NSARM (loc. 40.2.3 #1979-147.285); p.51 NSARM (loc. 42.18 #1979-147.209)(Artist: William Bartlett); p.52 ARHSM (Artist: David Macintosh); p.53 MMA (MP300.40.1; Neg 12,691; M79.47.7); p.54 top MMA (MP300.33.1; Neg 7136); p.54 bottom right MMA (MP300.3.2; Neg 14,077); p.54 bottom left YCM (PH 62L 19,20); p.55 top MMA (MP300.12.2; Neg 2722); p.55 bottom right MMA (MP 300.9.13; Neg 6755); p.55 bottom left ARHSM; p.56 MMA; p.57 NBM; p.58 ARHSM (Section I Photographs #10); p.58 ARHSM (Artist: David Macintosh); p.59 ARHSM (Artist: David Macintosh); p.60 Hugh M.D. MacNeil (artist: David Macintosh); p.61 Hugh M.D. MacNeil (Artist: David Macintosh); p.62 MMA (MP2.64.1); p.63 MMA (MP1.67.2 Neg 15,578); p.64 MMA; p.65 top DUA (MacMechan Collection; PG 2-7 p. 83); p.65 bottom DUA (MacMechan Collection; PG 2-7106); p.66 NSARM.

Chapter 4: p.68 MMA p.69 NSARM (1979-147.230)(Artist: Joseph Comingo); p.70 YCM (Artist: Sarah Bond Farish); p.71 top Artist: Jennie Morrow; p.71 bottom YCM (PH-12-Killam-4); p.72 top YCM; p. p.72 bottom YCM (PH-10-Killam-1); p.73YCM (PH-28-76); p.74 top YCM; p.74 bottom YCM (PH10-Parker-5); p.75YCM (PH10-Burrell-Johnson-17a); p.76 top YCM; p.76 bottom right YCM (PH-31-7-Grand); p.76 bottom left YCM; p.77 YCM; p.78 top MMA (FWW T68); p.78 bottom right YCM (Ph=62-Iranian (2)); p.78 bottom left YCM (PH-62-N(1)); p.79 top left YCM (PH-62-Iranian(4)); p.79 right MMA (MP1.182.44; Neg 2,840; Frederick William Wallace Collection T 109); p.79 bottom left YCM (Ph-62-Iranian (7)); p.80 YCM; p.81 YCM; p. 82 YCM; p. 83 left YCM (Iranian (8) Ph-62-I-18); p. 83 centre YCM; p.83 right NBM; p.86 MMA (MP1.103.2; N-23.916); p.87 YCM.

Chapter 5: p. 89 NSARM (loc. 42.37 #1979-147.505); p.90 NBM; p.91 NBM; p.92 NBM; p.93 NBM; p.94 NBM; p.95 NSARM (loc. 40.33 #1979-147.929); p.96 Charles A. Armour and Thomas Lackey, Sailing Ships of the Maritimes (McGraw-Hill Ryerson, 1975), p. 153; p.97 NBM; p.98 NBM; p. 99 NBM; p.100 bottom, NBM; top, MMA (MP1.102.1a; Frederick William Wallace Collection); p. 101 top NBM; p. 101 bottom MMA (MP2.126.4); p.102 top NBM; p.102 bottom NBM; p. 103 left MMA (MP218.1.1a; Wilson photo); p.104 NBM; p.105 McCord Museum (Notman Archives; 1-48435).

Chapter 6: p.106 NSARM (Artist: Albert G. Hoit); p.107 NSARM (1979-147.851; Artist: William Eager); p.108 Melvin Maddocks, The Great Liners (Time-Life Books, 1978), p.19; p.109 MMA; p.110 Capt. Ronald W. Warwick, QE2 (W. W. Norton, 1993), p.31; p.111 MMA (Artist: John O'Brien).

Chapter 7: p.115 NSARM (Places-Lunenburg Harbour 1898 F237/01); p.116 MMA (MP 11.1.42 N 4117); p.117 MMA (MP 10.37.1A; Neg 25,029); p.118 MMA (MP10.55.30; Neg 4929; Frederick William Wallace Collection); p.119 MMA (MP400.173.5; Neg 22,274; Frederick William Wallace Collection N10); p.122 left MMA (MP10.54.32; Neg 21,164; Frederick William Wallace Collection C47); p.122 right MMA (MP10.157.27; Neg 20,960; Frederick William Wallace Collection B5); p.123 MMA (MP10.55.52; Neg 21,168; Frederick William Wallace Collection A12); p.124 left FMA; p.125 Knickles Studio; p.127 MMA (MP10.88.2; Neg 3079; Frederick William Wallace Collection); p.128 MMA (MP300.16.17; Neg 3084; Frederick William Wallace Collection); p.129 MMA (MP11.1.6; Neg 17,198); p.130 MMA; p.131 Knickles Studio.

Chapter 8: p.134 Norman Munroe; p.135 Pictou Recreation, Tourism and Culture (artist: David MacIntosh); p.136 Norman Munroe; pp.142-3 Hugh M.D. MacNeil.

Photography of artifacts at museums in Avondale, Halifax, Lunenburg and Yarmouth: Julian Beveridge. Photography: pp. 37, 46, 141 Keith Vaughan.

Formac Publishing Company Limited acknowledges the support of the Cultural Affairs Section, Nova Scotia Department of Tourism and Culture. We acknowledge the financial support of the Government of Canada through the Book Publishing Industry Development Program (BPIDP) for our publishing activities.
We acknowledge the support of the Canada Council for the Arts for our publishing program.

Page 1: *John A. Harvie*
Cover: Construction of the *Parthena*, Avondale. Artist: David MacIntosh
Illustration research: Shelagh Mackenzie
Illustration selection: Roger Marsters

Canadian Cataloguing in Publication Data

Spicer, Stanley T., 1924-
The age of sail: the master shipbuilders of the Maritimes

Includes bibliography and index
ISBN 0-88780-539-6
1. Shipbuilding—Maritime Provinces—History—19th century.
2. Sailing ships—Maritime Provinces — History — 19th century.
3. Shipbuilding industry—Maritime Provinces-History—19th century.
I. Title
VM27.M37S59 2001   338.4'762382'009715 C2001-903035-5

Formac Publishing Company Limited
5502 Atlantic Street
Halifax, Nova Scotia B3H 1G4
www.formac.ca
Printed and bound in Canada

Contents

ACKNOWLEDGEMENTS

My deepest gratitude is expressed to these institutions and individuals who contributed so much to this work and who strive to perpetuate the story of the Age of Sail in the Maritime provinces:

Avon River Heritage Museum, Newport Landing (Avondale), Nova Scotia—Vice Admiral (Ret'd.) Hugh M.D. MacNeil, Andrew Fisher, Darrell Burke, George R. Mounce, Andrew Fisher and Robin Bates; Fisheries Museum of the Atlantic, Lunenburg, Nova Scotia—James Tupper, Sue Ann Mersey and Ralph Getson; Maritime Museum of the Atlantic, Halifax, Nova Scotia—Michael Murray, Marven Moore and Dan Conlin; Miramichi Natural History Museum, Miramichi, New Brunswick—Amy Wheaton and Marc Noel; New Brunswick Museum, Saint John, New Brunswick—Gary Hughes, Regina Martin, Felicity Osepchook and Peter Larocque; P.E.I. Museum and Heritage Foundation, Charlottetown, Prince Edward Island—Boyde Beck; Public Archives of Prince Edward Island, Charlottetown, Prince Edward Island—Marilyn Bell and staff; Yarmouth County Museum, Yarmouth, Nova Scotia—Eric Ruff, Laura Bradley, Janice Stelma and Vaughan Bullerwell.

Then there are individuals who have gone above and beyond in providing information essential to the pages that follow: Captain Owen Creaser, Riverport, Nova Scotia; Robert Elliott, Saint John, New Brunswick; Robert Killam, Yarmouth, Nova Scotia; David Knickle, Lunenburg, Nova Scotia; Karen Rafuse, Lunenburg, Nova Scotia

Appreciation is expressed to editor Elizabeth Eve and publisher James Lorimer for their encouragement and professional guidance.

Finally, the assistance provided by my wife Gwen in researching and organizing material made this book possible.

Stanley Spicer
Spencers Island
Nova Scotia
2001

DEDICATION

To Dr. Blake O'Brien, Fredericton, New Brunswick
A son of the Miramichi and a friend for 60 years

INTRODUCTION

During the Tall Ships' visit to Halifax in 2000, thousands of people lined the city's waterfront to view the parade of sailing vessels that circuited the harbour and then headed out to the Atlantic. In an age of gargantuan container ships, the chance to see the billowing sails and elegant lines of vessels, large and small, old and new, was an opportunity too good to pass up. People came from many parts of the continent and from overseas to get a taste of living history. They admired the detailed woodwork, the complex rigging and the handpowered machinery that characterize sail power.

It was ships that brought people from Europe to the Maritimes, and it was timber and other raw products that provided them a reason to stay and build flourishing communities. Fortunes were made in the forests of North America with the almost endless supply of timber for shipbuilders in the United Kingdom. In a matter of time, as an adjunct to the logging and lumber trade, entrepreneurs began constructing vessels along rivers, such as the Miramichi and the Saint John, and in

suitable coastal locations, such as Murray River, Prince Edward Island, and St. Martin's, New Brunswick. Shipbuilding and shipowning quickly took shape in many parts of the region.

Between 1830 and 1920 untold numbers of sailing vessels were built in coastal communities of the Maritime provinces. Around the Bay of Fundy alone, some 8000 vessels were launched, all large enough to travel the world's oceans and all powered by wind. Prince Edward Island shipbuilders produced more than 4000. By the end of the nineteenth century, approximately 26,000 vessels had been built, some for local shipowners, many for overseas buyers.

This book reveals the geographic and economic scope of the shipbuilding and shipowning industry. In the Miramichi, the rambunctious Joseph Cunard was at the centre of a logging and shipbuilding business that helped bring wealth and immigrants to northeastern New Brunswick. The shipbuilders of Prince Edward Island were more often funded by brokers such as James Peake and James Yeo, who sold their large vessels to British buyers. In rural Nova Scotia, on the tidal rivers that run into Minas Basin, families like the Moshers and Mounces took control of both the building and the sailing of large commercial vessels, which carried goods between markets around the world. Similarly, in Saint John and Yarmouth the Troops and the Killams, respectively, assembled large fleets, bringing economic booms to their local communities, of which the legacies can still be seen today. Halifax-born Samuel Cunard is doubtless the shipbuilding entrepreneur whose legacy outgrew and outlasted all of his countrymen.

The spirit of the golden age of sail continues in the Wind, Wood and Sail exhibit in Saint John, a collaboration of the New Brunswick Museum and Parks Canada, in the Age of Sail exhibit at the Maritime Museum of the Atlantic in Halifax, at the Avon River Heritage Society Museum at Newport Landing and at the Fisheries Museum in Lunenburg. The respect for tradition in craftsmanship and in marine matters has also lead to the present-day building of replicas in Maritime shipyards. In reconstructing the *Hector*, the *Bluenose II*, the *Avon Spirit*, the *Bounty*, and the *Rose*, the combination of both graceful design and practical usage, which go into constructing working wooden sailing vessels, has been rediscovered by many skilled craftsmen, including carpenters and blacksmiths. Of course, the original purpose of these vessels has been displaced: the immigrant ship, the fishing vessel, and the naval frigate are now visitor attractions in various ports around the world.

Masts did not vanish overnight from the east coast harbours. The demise of square-rigged sailing vessels coincided with the turn of the century, but commercial schooners continued in service through the 1920s and 1930s. Ambitious entrepreneurs, such as the Cunards, moved to Britain; other builders stayed in their communities and, like Smith and Rhuland, adapted their boatbuilding skills to current needs. Still others invested in the railways. Shipbuilding brought technology and industry to the region. In the harbours where timber could be floated downriver to the shoreline, settlers founded communities that flourished into towns, built small saw mills that turned into factories, wharves that grew into busy ports. The chapters in this book introduce a few of the families who helped make the Age of Sail in the Maritimes a time of prosperity and nation-building.

Stanley T. Spicer
September 2001

Opposite: Yarmouth harbour, 1829.
Above: Hanging a plank on a vessel under construction.

Chapter One

THE MIRAMICHI
AND JOSEPH CUNARD

When it became public that Joseph Cunard's business empire had crumbled, an angry mob gathered on Chatham's Water Street. Panic engulfed the crowd; hundreds of men would almost certainly be put out of work; families would become destitute. There were shouts of "Shoot Cunard!" But the object of their rage faced the people impassively. Standing over six feet tall and weighing more than 200 pounds, with a loaded pistol stuck in each high boot, Cunard was an impressive figure. He smiled and roared, "Let me see the man that will shoot Cunard." The crowd slowly melted away.

In only twenty-five years, Cunard had managed to bring a wealth of industry to the Miramichi region and at the same time stir up a lot of discontent. The Cunards descended from German immigrants who

Joseph Cunard, 1797-1865, brother of Samuel Cunard.

moved to Philadelphia sometime in the mid-seventeenth century. During the American Revolution, Robert, Joseph's grandfather, served with the British and came to Saint John as a Loyalist refugee in 1783. His son Abraham moved to Halifax and established a shipping firm with his own eldest son, Samuel, under the name A. Cunard and Company. Such were young Samuel Cunard's business talents that by 1820 the operation was known as S. Cunard and Company, a name that very soon became known in many parts of the world.

By the mid-1820s Cunard was ready to expand his lumber and shipping interests to the Miramichi and he dispatched his younger brothers—Joseph, Henry and John—to the area for that purpose.

John did not stay, but the other two young men, with Samuel Cunard's financial backing, expanded and developed both the lumber business and shipyards.

The Miramichi River cuts deep into the heartland of New Brunswick. Flowing in an approximate southwest-northeast direction, it opens into Miramichi Bay on the Gulf of St. Lawrence about 100 kilometres west of North Cape on Prince Edward Island

Trees were felled and taken out of the forest in winter because the frozen ground was comparatively easier to traverse than the mud in spring and fall. This early lithograph shows how trees were felled in the early days of lumbering.

and some 160 kilometres north of Moncton. In the earliest years of the nineteenth century, the magnificent forests and the broad rivers that flowed through them were ideal territory for logging. Settlers in the area were already prospering from the lumber trade before the Cunards arrived.

As early as 1819, of the more than 1500 British vessels engaged in the North American timber trade, about 300 loaded on the Miramichi River. In the period between 1815 and 1824, during the shipping season, the Miramichi was frequently crowded with more than 100 square-rigged vessels loading timber.

The first known vessel built on the shores of the Miramichi was William Davidson's schooner *Miramichi*, launched in 1773. However, shipbuilding did not develop into a steady source of employment until the 1820s. The first shipyards were located on the shores of Miramichi Bay at Neguac and Bay du Vin and along both sides of the river.

During the era of wooden shipbuilding there were at least two dozen shipyards on the river, many of them under successive ownership. Among the more prominent builders were

William Fiddes, Joseph Russell—from whom Cunard acquired his yard at England's Hollow—and William Abrams, who built some two dozen vessels on the north shore of the river east of Newcastle. Other builders included Gilmour and Rankin (who were effective opponents of Cunard), John Harley and the firm of Johnson and Mackie.

Seldom are siblings as disparate as the Cunard brothers: Samuel was a business genius and both cautious and ambitious; Joseph was boisterous, vain and domineering; and Henry was reclusive and evidently out of place in the rough-and-ready, give-and-take of the nineteenth-century business world.

The year following the Cunard brothers' arrival, the Great Miramichi Fire of 1825 swept through the town of Newcastle and destroyed many businesses and homes. An abnormally dry summer that year, forest fires had frequently flared up. The conflagration that erupted on October 7 destroyed Newcastle, Douglastown and the north side of the Miramichi River down to Burnt Church. Firefighting equipment was primitive and inadequate for a fire this fierce. By the time the fire was extinguished, it had consumed 6000 square miles of forest and had caused the death of

Informed by generations of practice, experienced shipbuilders saw woodlands as an inexhaustible source of specialized ship timbers—frames, keel timbers, ships' knees— whose natural shapes gave wooden vessels great strength in their unequal battle with the immense power of the sea.

Log jams were a common sight in the nineteenth century, when the region's rivers were the main highways of a hugely profitable timber trade. On the Miramichi and elsewhere timber provided both the raw materials for shipbuilding and the chief cargo for export to Europe.

Raftsmen had the delicate job of shepherding timber to sawmills at the head of navigable water. This early watercolour suggests just how nimble these men could be.

160 people. One of Joseph Cunard's first responsibilities was to serve on the relief committee that assisted hundreds of destitute citizens.

More civic appointments followed. Joseph was appointed Justice of the Peace for Northumberland County and named Commissioner of Lighthouses. In 1828, he was elected a member of the provincial Legislative Assembly and won re-election in 1830. Eight years later,

Raw logs were channelled into sawmills where they were cut into square timbers or deals—rough planks—for export. Here several ocean-going barques lie alongside a mill awaiting their cargos.

A rare interior photograph of a sawmill in the late nineteenth century. The simplicity of sawmill technology made the industry highly mobile, able to set up wherever there was timber and water enough to float it.

Fredericton, c. 1842, engraving by William Bartlett. View from across the river.

Barques drying sail while loading at Sinclair's Mill, near Newcastle. In the foreground are stacked softwood deals, the standard commodity of the Miramichi timber trade.

was meteoric. Within a few years, its mercantile empire included stores in Newcastle, Chatham, Bathurst, Shippegan, Kouchibouguac and Richibucto. Newspaper advertisements proclaimed that these stores offered groceries, hardware, dry goods, liquor, clothing and tools. In addition, the company obtained vast areas of forest reserves on the Northwest Miramichi and Big Nepisiguit rivers in return for promises to clear obstacles from the river bottom, to deepen Bathurst's harbour and to build sluices

In the early 1830s, Chatham was poised to expand into a thriving town. With a population of just less than 10,000, it nevertheless had three schools, eight merchants, a weekly newspaper, a post office and a market.

Having already established himself as a community leader, it was only fitting that Joseph Cunard's marriage to Mary Peters in 1833 was presided over by the Anglican bishop of Nova Scotia who happened to be in the area at the time. To further cement his stature, that same year Cunard arranged for the construction of a suitable mansion. Unfortunately, all that remains is a description that defines his grandiose dreams:

when he joined the provincial Executive Council, he was described by the Lieutenant-Governor as "one of the most wealthy and influential merchants in the province."

The rise of J. Cunard and Company in the local business world

Huge fireplaces heated the four lower rooms—on the second floor across the whole front was the Ball Room, with folded panelling to divide it when

A view over the rooftops of the tidy wooden town of Newcastle, looking towards the deep-water shipping in the busy Miramichi River beyond.

Barques loading timber at Ritchies' Wharf in Newcastle, in the 1890s. In the late nineteenth century new technologies—for example, the steam tug in the foreground—were increasingly used to maintain the profitability of this traditional industry.

wished. The third floor had a vaulted high ceiling which led to a small balcony. Here Cunard could gaze out on his estate with the semi-circular driveway, his gardens, flowers, coachmen and the beautiful peacocks roaming the manicured grounds.

During his second decade in Chatham, Cunard rapidly expanded his business holdings. In 1835, construction began on a sawmill, a large two-storey structure with an engine house alongside and long wharves jutting out into the river. Three years later, he added a grist mill, despite the admonitions of his brother Samuel, who wrote:

I am sorry to find that you have been adding a large building to the Steam Mill. It increases the risk of fire where such an immense property is at stake beside the additional Capital sunk in this confounded Undertaking.

Unlike his brothers, who were more cautious and thoughtful in nature, Joseph leaned heavily toward extravagance and hasty decisions. It is easy to picture this big man on his huge horse galloping from town to town and from worksite to worksite supervising the various projects with a dictatorial air.

In the late 1830s, Henry Cunard left the company, concentrating on his own business interests and retiring to his estate to live as a gentleman farmer. This left Joseph with the responsibility for the Cunards' shipbuilding interests in northeastern New Brunswick.

Aside from the vessels built in Chatham in 1828 and 1829, the major expansion of Joseph's shipbuilding interest started in 1839 when he acquired the Joseph Russell shipyard at England's Hollow just east of Chatham. Simultaneously, he began building vessels to the north in Bathurst and to the south in Kent County, principally at Kouchibouguac.

Records suggest that he was the pioneer shipbuilder in the Bathurst area, although he was soon followed by others such as George and Alfred Smith, John Woolner, Ferguson, Rankin and Company—who were allied with Gilmour and Rankin on the Miramichi—John A. Meahan and John E. O'Brien. At least 100 vessels appear to have been launched in the Bathurst area by the various builders in the mid-nineteenth century.

In Kent County, which was an even more prolific shipbuilding centre, Cunard was only a minor player. Other builders who were responsible for more than 200 vessels emerging from yards in the area included the Jardines, George K. McLeod, J.W. Holderness and L.P.W. DesBrisay.

Joseph Cunard's remarkable career as a shipbuilder was short-lived and prolific. In less than a decade, he launched some eight vessels in Kent County, twenty-four in Bathurst and more than forty at England's Hollow. Such was his rate of production that in Cunard's Bathurst yard, he launched the barques *Susan* and *Caroline* on the same day in November of 1839, and a year later he launched two more barques—the *General Wiltshire* and the *Lord Keane*—from the same place on the same day. In one week in 1846, he launched the barque *Hydaspes* in Bathurst, the schooner *Velocity* in Abbyland at Kouchibouguac and, in Chatham, the steamer *Velocity*, believed to be the first steam-driven vessel built on the Miramichi.

Most of the Cunard vessels were built for the British market and sailed without being registered in Canada. It was a process variously known as "going home under certificate" or sailing under a "governor's pass."

Cunard did not believe in wasting time either in building his vessels or in launching them. His barque *Guatemala* was launched on the afternoon of August 24, 1844. One week later, it had cleared the river for Britain after being masted and rigged and, in three days, loaded with 330,000 deals, 5000 deal ends, 27 tons of birch timbers and other wood products. The *Guatemala* was sold in Liverpool, England.

Another of Cunard's vessels is worthy of special mention. Also launched in 1844, the *Swordfish* was one of the better-known vessels to come out of the Miramichi. This 341-ton barque was built as a

Workers enjoying a rare moment of calm amidst the bustle of Ritchies' Wharf, Newcastle. In the foreground a small coastal schooner loads timber, perhaps for one of the growing cities of eastern North America.

packet ship for the Brazil trade out of Liverpool. The *Chatham Gleaner* claimed that "for beauty of model and style of workmanship we have seldom seen her equal."

In 1845, the *Swordfish* sailed from Liverpool to Pernambuco in twenty-five days, the shortest passage on record, even though it was becalmed for three days. Later that same year, it made another extraordinary passage from Bahia to Liverpool in twenty-two days. The *Swordfish* was abandoned at sea, sinking on a voyage from Pernambuco to Liverpool in 1852.

One of Joseph Cunard's holdings played a significant role in the horrific accounts of the immigrant ships, or "coffin ships," that brought mostly Irish families to the Miramichi area.

Opposite: An 1826 painting of Beaubairs Island, site of prominent Miramichi builder Joseph Russell's shipyard, showing a remarkable variety of shipping on the river. In addition to three-masted ocean-going ships and timber rafts, the scene is busy with a variety of small craft including, at left, a small colonial ketch and, in the foreground, a high-sided native bark canoe.

Barques alongside and at anchor in Chatham. The placid weather that gives this photograph such picturesque charm also ensures that the steam tug St. Nicholas, *foreground, will have a busy day getting becalmed vessels underway.*

By the 1840s, economic conditions in Ireland were so bad that thousands decided to make a fresh start in North America. The few who could afford cabins sailed in comfort; the majority who could only afford to travel steerage class suffered indescribable privation. They were packed into unventilated holds amid vermin, filth and with a minimum of food. Typhus and cholera were rampant on these vessels, which often took several weeks to cross the Atlantic. It soon became necessary to provide a quarantine station; Middle Island, owned by Cunard, was the selected site.

One June day in 1847, a vessel arrived from Dublin. The ship had departed with 467 passengers, but by the time it arrived at Middle Island, 117 had died en route and another hundred were extremely ill. Of those, forty died and were buried on the island. Vessel after vessel arrived with sick and dying passengers. At one point, there were 350 people quarantined on the island. Among the victims was John Vondy, a young doctor who volunteered to administer to the sick on Middle Island. He succumbed to the disease himself and died in July of 1847 at the age of twenty-six.

At the height of his career in eastern New Brunswick, Joseph Cunard employed about 2000 people. He dominated Chatham's political and business life, and he craved and expected a certain amount of adulation and respect. The *Chatham Gleaner*

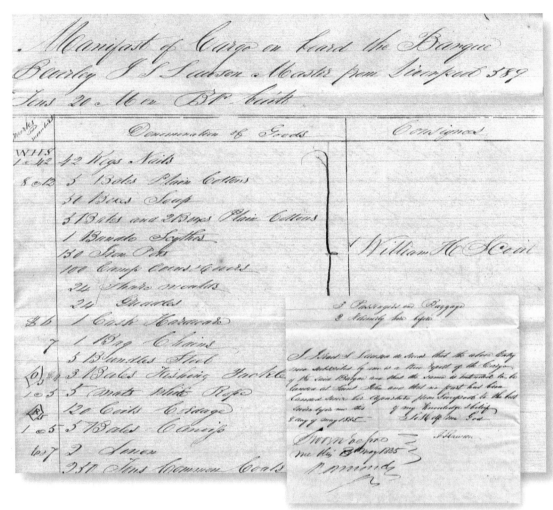

A ship's manifest showing the range of goods typically carried by deep-water ships in the nineteenth century.

Ships in the timber trade were typically built with special ports in the bow to ease loading. Here, workers are shown winching squared timber through such a port, which will be closed and re-caulked before departure.

described the welcome to accorded Cunard following his return from an extended trip:

On a fine day in September, Cunard having been absent for two months, was now returning home. As his boat was seen rounding Middle Island, which at one time he also owned, several gun salutes were fired from near his mill. By the time his boat landed, a large crowd had gathered to give three cheers for their benefactor.

The paper did not mention that Cunard had sent a messenger on ahead to announce the estimated time of his arrival.

Widespread economic depression in 1842 could have ruined Cunard. For several years he had been borrowing heavily from various local merchants, including Michael Samuel, who expressed fears of losing upwards of $50,000 if Cunard went under. But Cunard survived this downturn and, despite his financial problems, continued to build ships. In fact, 1846 was his peak year. While he launched only one vessel at Kouchibouguac, the barque *Abbyland*, he produced four in Bathurst and three barques, a schooner and the aforementioned steamer *Velocity* in Chatham; the following year he launched another eight vessels. Inevitably, his demise came quickly; the launch of the barque *Northumberland* at England's Hollow in 1848 signalled the end.

Several things contributed to Cunard's downfall. For years, he had fostered a rivalry with Gilmour, Rankin and Company, shipbuilders on the other side of the Miramichi River. Much of the dispute centred around ownership of timber reserves. In the end, after long drawn-out legal battles and in spite of Cunard's economic and social status, his rivals won the case. This cost him dearly. In addition to the widespread economic depression, Cunard's personal extravagance and imprudent business practices also played a large part in his demise. It was said that farmers could bring produce into Cunard's stores and be paid several times over simply by going from clerk to clerk with their accounts.

The day came in December 1847 when Joseph Cunard could no longer meet his financial obligations and he declared bankruptcy. For some months, this news was not public knowledge, and by the time it became so, in 1848, the Miramichi area was in the grip of serious economic trouble.

Sawmill with an adjacent boatyard in a typical rural New Brunswick community.

Unemployment was high and men were leaving in droves for New England and Quebec. Chatham was in despair and, some anonymous scribe wrote:

At dark on the Richibucto Road
No cannons boomed or beacons glowed,
A man rode alone through the gathering night,
With the frogs for band and the stars for light.
Wrapped in his cloak, with his head bent down,
Joe Cunard is leaving town.

In fact, even after the angry citizens confronted him on Water Street in 1848, he did no such thing—at least not immediately. Cunard stayed in Chatham to settle his affairs. The thousands of acres of timberlands he owned or had leased throughout Northumberland, Kent and Gloucester counties were disposed of to help settle his debts. It took until 1871, some six years after his death,

before all of his debts were erased, including those of one of his largest creditors, his brother Samuel.

Although a general shipbuilding boom began in 1850 and brought life back to the Miramichi, it was too late for Cunard. A sudden demand for vessels to carry emigrants to Australia, to transport troops and supplies to the Crimea and to take fortune-seekers around Cape Horn to the California gold fields put the Miramichi back on the road to prosperity.

By this time, Joseph Cunard had sailed to Liverpool, England, where he became a partner in Cunard, Munn and Company, Commission Merchants. A few years later the company became Cunard, Brett and Austin, and still later Cunard, Wilson and Company.

At the Liverpool Exchange he became a general favourite and had a reputation as a kindhearted and genial gentleman, full of stories and always ready to share his knowledge and experience. Clearly, he had turned his considerable charm on to the Liverpool business community.

Sometime before his death he was knighted and on January 16, 1865, his colourful and tempestuous life ended after a short illness; he was sixty-six. Even his burial was grand. He was buried in three coffins: an inner shell enclosed in a lead coffin and an outer coffin of oak.

During his time on the Miramichi, Joseph Cunard came to be loved and hated, admired and feared. He was as generous as he was tight-fisted, as kind as he was ruthless. He has been gone from the Miramichi for a century and a half, but such was his style that the Cunard name will forever be associated with the area.

Chapter Two

THE PEAKES OF PRINCE EDWARD ISLAND

When John Peters launched the schooner *St. Patrick* at Rustico in May 1787, he had no way of knowing that it was the first of thousands of vessels that would be built on Prince Edward Island during the Maritimes' Age of Sail.

No records have survived that show the extent of shipbuilding prior to this date, but in 1787, after the British government required all decked vessels to be registered, the brig *Speedwell*, weighing 104 tons, was launched in New London for John Cambridge, a Charlottetown shipowner. These launchings were signs that a new industry bringing employment and prosperity to the island was well underway.

Shipbuilding and shipowning began on Prince Edward Island for the same reasons they were initiated elsewhere on Canada's East Coast. Roads were so few and so poor that water was the most feasible route for communication and transportation. Not only were ships the sole way to move timber and fish to markets but they also brought manufactured goods to the growing towns and villages on the Island.

The early shipbuilders had several advantages, suitable sites were abundant around the coast, and the raw materials were readily at hand. The shipbuilding industry expanded rapidly, from about 50

vessels in the first decade of the nineteenth century to more than 370 by the 1820s. Indeed, launchings became so commonplace that they attracted little attention from the press. If they were mentioned at all, it was similar to the following report, which appeared in the Charlottetown *Colonial Herald* on September 5, 1840:

On Wednesday, 31st ultimo from the shipyard of Messrs. Orr, New Glasgow, a fine copper-fastened schooner called the Regina. *This is the fifth vessel launched from that establishment for Mr. Peake in the short space of twelve months.*

The facilities necessary to build these vessels were rudimentary. The first requirement was a site adjacent to water where the land gradually sloped down to the water's edge and with water deep enough to float a vessel. The foundation was provided by a series of massive timbers embedded in the earth, parallel to the water's edge and running inland like railway ties somewhat longer than the proposed vessel's length. On these timbers, large blocks were constructed to support the keel.

Until the advent of sawmills, a saw pit was dug, about eight or nine feet deep. The logs were dragged over the pit, and with one man on top of the log and another at the bottom of the pit—one on each end of a long saw—the two produced the planks for the vessel. Since these planks could be anywhere from two to six inches thick, and had to be bent and twisted to conform to the shape of the hull, a steam box was needed to soften the planks.

Other facilities in the smaller shipyards included a loft, where full-sized plans could be laid down for the component parts of the vessel such as the stem, sternpost and frames. A blacksmith's shop, which was either part of the yard or close to it, produced ironwork such as anchors, mast bands and fastenings. Finally a shed to store tools and materials completed the yard. Larger shipyards included such specialists as blockmakers and sailmakers, carvers for figureheads and wheels and, possibly, accommodation for itinerant shipwrights.

Making sails for the old square-riggers and schooners was a craft that was often handed down from father to son. Before the introduction of sewing machines, sail-makers sat side by side on long benches. Sails were made by sewing together long panels of cotton canvas, each of which was twenty-two inches wide.

Traditional sailmaker's bench (above) and tools from a ditty bag (below), on display at the Maritime Museum of the Atlantic, Halifax.

Experienced men sewing four stitches to the inch could cover twenty yards per hour; this expertise was acquired in a five-year apprenticeship. Canvas, which replaced flax in the nineteenth century because it could better hold its shape, came in various weights, the heavier used on the larger sails, the lighter on the smaller ones. The cut of each sail was very precisely measured; the vessel's performance depended on one sail properly filling with wind and working in conjunction with the other. Heavy canvas sails were worthy opponents for sailors trying to furl them in gale-force winds or in wintry conditions—lost fingernails were a badge of the sailors' trade.

A leading sail-making business employed upwards of twenty men working twelve-hour days, six days per week. A business of this size could turn out complete sails for a full-rigged ship in four weeks, and such a vessel would require approximately 10,000 yards of canvas for its sails.

Vessels built on Prince Edward Island were designed to meet the needs of the markets they served. For decades, many were sold to Newfoundland as boats for the seal hunt, the Labrador fishery and coastal trading. These tended to be rigged either as schooners, brigs or brigantines, and were a suitable size for coastal conditions.

A view of the harbour and town of Charlottetown in the nineteenth century. Charlottetown was a bustling port handling the colony's export staples: agricultural produce, salt fish, and the schooners, brigs, brigantines, and barques that were in great demand both locally and in Newfoundland and the United Kingdom.

Many more were sent to the British Isles, to use in the coastal, Baltic and North European trades. After launching, the vessels would carry a cargo—often timber—to Britain. At times there were specialized demands, such as in the 1840s when the British railway system needed rail ties, resulting in larger vessels loaded with suitable timber being sent across the Atlantic. Another demand arose with the outbreak of the Crimean War, when Britain needed transports for men and supplies.

Some Island-built vessels were sold to buyers in the other Maritime provinces, while others were owned by Islanders who shipped farm produce, fish and livestock to the West Indies, Brazil, Newfoundland and ports on the eastern seaboard of the United States.

The rate of producing vessels followed a well-defined curve throughout the nineteenth century. Between 1796 and 1810, there were 71 vessels launched; in the 1830s, 504 vessels were registered. The peak production period was the 1860s, when 913 were put to sea, after which shipbuilding declined sharply to 545 vessels in the 1870s

and only 129 in the 1880s.

While Island vessels tended to be smaller than those built in Nova Scotia and New Brunswick, there were exceptions. The largest sailing vessel ever built on the Island was James Duncan's *Ethel*, launched in Charlottetown in 1858. At 1795 tons, the *Ethel* ranks among the largest vessels ever built in the Maritimes.

In shipbuilding there is a tendency to confuse the terms "builder" and "owner." A builder might be the master builder who supervised the day-to-day construction of a vessel, or it might refer to the person who owned the shipyard and employed a master builder. The owners financed the vessel's construction and assumed ownership after launching. Often, the builder who owned his shipyard would build a vessel for his own use, thus becoming both builder and owner. Sometimes owners who had financed a vessel's construction but had had nothing to do with the building process were listed on the vessel's register as the builder, which has caused problems in trying to establish the facts about ownership and construction.

Among the notable builders on Prince Edward Island were two families, the Orrs, principally of New Glasgow, and the Coffins, who did much of their shipbuilding at Mount Stewart. However, if there was one name that was dominant as both a builder and owner on Prince Edward Island, it was Yeo.

James Yeo Sr. began his business life dealing in lumber and operating a general store in Port Hill. Moving into shipbuilding, he

A brigantine nearing completion at Cardigan in the 1890s, clearly showing the simplicity of shipyards in many Island communities.

The tern (three-masted) schooner Empress, *built at Montague. Like the many brigs and brigantines launched from P.E.I. yards, tern schooners were employed mostly in the coastal trade, particularly along the American seaboard and in the Caribbean. Typically, the* Empress *was ultimately transferred to Barbadian registry.*

Islanders' shipbuilding skills were also employed in building hundreds of small vessels for the local fisheries. Here schooner-rigged lobster boats are hauled up on the shingle beach at Black Marsh.

launched his first vessel in 1833 and rapidly expanded his operations. The Yeo shipyard became one of the largest on the Island, including all the requisite facilities along with a sail loft, provisions for riggers and accommodations for the workmen.

In 1845, James Yeo sent his son William to Appledore, England, where he served as his father's agent. His other sons, James Jr. and John, were also shipbuilders, as was James's son-in-law, William Richards. Richards was a master mariner who retired from the sea to build vessels, first with the Yeos and later on his own, at Bideford. The extended Yeo family is credited with building more than 300 vessels.

Other shipowners were James and Andrew Duncan of Charlottetown, who operated a shipyard but also had vessels built by others. Daniel Brenan, also of Charlottetown, financed the building of some twenty vessels between 1845 and 1859. James C. Pope of Summerside was both a shipbuilder and owner. Between 1845 and 1859, these

A coastal schooner alongside at Murray Harbour. This trim little vessel looks entirely at home among the neat wooden frame houses, and indeed could have been built by the same hands.

Green Park, the estate of James Yeo, Jr. at Port Hill, P.E.I., built in 1865. The inset shows the barque Ponemah *in frame. Yeo's house and shipyard have been preserved as the Green Park Shipbuilding Museum.*

James Yeo Sr., patriarch of the Yeo shipbuilding clan.

three men built or financed a total of 90 vessels of which 74 were destined for British buyers.

Another prominent name in shipbuilding was Peake. James Peake Sr. created a highly successful business, which he passed on to his son. Their story begins in the late 1820s, when James Ellis Peake arrived in Charlottetown from his native Plymouth, England. He began business slowly, building only one vessel in 1829 and another in 1830. From then on, the number of vessels he owned in whole or in part increased rapidly. The builders he favoured and the locations of their shipyards covered much of the Island: Joshua Dyrong (or Doiron) of Rustico, Arthur and Thomas Owen of Three Rivers, and Thomas Richard of Murray Harbour were among his early builders. Later, he also had vessels built by Robert and William Orr of New Glasgow, John Pippy of Charlottetown, Thomas Perkins of Souris, Lemuel Owen of Cardigan and Andrew Bell of New London.

Consistent with the prevailing size of local vessels, James Peake's crafts tended to be smaller than those produced elsewhere. Among his largest were two barques, *Ajax* and *Agnes*, launched in 1846 and 1851, respectively, each less than 550 tons, while his smallest, such as the schooners *Charlotte* and *Chase*, measured less than 50 tons.

Peake was fortunate to lose relatively few vessels at sea, mainly because he sold vessels quickly—some in Newfoundland, a few

Yeo House, Port Hill. The elaborate gingerbread and refined interior woodwork reflect the shipbuilding concerns of its builder. The widow's walk, a feature typical of houses in many Maritime communities, continues to overlook the site of James Yeo Jr.'s shipyard at the head of Campbell Creek.

The Bank of Prince Edward Island, Charlottetown, founded by James Peake Sr.

elsewhere, but the majority in the British Isles. He rarely kept a vessel more than a few years, and he often sold them the same year in which they were launched.

It isn't certain if he was seriously considering marriage at the time, but in 1835 Peake had a brick home built on Water Street in Charlottetown. The house, which is still standing, was located close to his wharves and business operations. In July 1837, he married Alice Brecken, a member of a prominent Island family. The union produced six children: daughters Elizabeth and Barbara and sons James Jr., George and Ralph, followed by daughter Fanny.

In the 1840s, Peake's business interests expanded rapidly. He had nearly seventy vessels built for his own account, purchased others and held mortgages on several more. Nearly all were sold in the British Isles, and one—the brig *Fanny*—departed Charlottetown on November 12, 1849, with more than fifty Islanders aboard, bound for the California gold fields. None, however, was believed to have struck it rich.

Throughout the early 1850s, Peake's business continued to flourish as new vessels were commissioned and launched. His waterfront properties expanded, and he achieved the status of one of the Island's foremost business leaders. But his health was beginning to fail, and in the fall of 1856 the family returned to Plymouth, England, to seek a cure. One of his last acts before departure was to assist in founding the Bank of Prince Edward Island. Peake's return to England did not have the desired effect, and on May 4, 1860, he passed away at the age of sixty-three.

During his years on Prince Edward Island, Peake had been involved in the ownership of some 150 vessels. About the time of his death, his waterfront holdings in Charlottetown included stores, warehouses, two large wharves, and at least two residential properties that were rented out. All of this was left for his widow and appointed trustees to manage, a responsibility which they capably carried out over the next few years.

In 1863, Peake's eldest son, twenty-one-year-old James Jr., returned to Charlottetown to take control of the family business. He was joined later by his brothers, George and Ralph.

Market Building, Queen's Square, Charlottetown in the 1860s. This imposing structure of rusticated sandstone reflects the enduring importance of agricultural produce to the Island's economy.

The three-masted barque Ralph B. Peake *built at Mount Stewart in 1876 and partly owned by James Peake Jr. along with his brothers George and Ralph. This formal portrait shows it at its best, with all sails set and pulling, with two seamen straining at the wheel and the captain scanning the horizon from the weather rail.*

James Peake Sr., prominent shipbuilder and merchant.

Soon after his arrival, young James and Daniel Hodgson, a trustee of his father's estate, became shipowners; between 1864 and 1866 they owned nearly a dozen vessels, including the brig *Edith Haviland* built at Morell in 1865. The vessel's name was a forerunner, for in 1866 James married Edith Constance Haviland, the daughter of Thomas Heath Haviland, a successful lawyer and prominent Island political figure.

The first year he was married, James and his brothers formed Peake Brothers and Company along with Thomas Handrahan, who brought considerable business experience to the firm, something the young Peakes still lacked. It was an opportune time to launch the company because the 1860s were the apex in shipbuilding on the Island. The steep, irreversible decline for the industry came on the heels of the cancellation of the Reciprocity Treaty with British North America in 1869, when Island vessels could no longer deliver duty-free goods to New England. Concurrently, the British demand for vessels fell off sharply for about a decade, and although the industry rebounded modestly, the sun was sinking on the wooden square-rigged sailing vessels.

The factors contributing to the demise of Island shipbuilding included British market conditions, which fluctuated rapidly during this time. The downturns that brought about lower demand for

James Peake Sr. built this house on Water St., Charlottetown, in 1835.

41

The brigantine Sela, *built at Cranberry Point in 1859, owned by James Peake Sr. and registered in the United Kingdom. Its workmanlike lines and versatile rig were well suited for the British coastal trade.*

Island vessels and lower freight rates became longer, while the occasional upswings became mere hiccups in the overall economic picture. Then the once-dependable Newfoundland market for vessels fell off, due in part to increased local shipbuilding activity.

Another major factor was the advent in Britain of iron sailing vessels, which not only lasted longer than the wooden hulls, but could also sail closer to the wind, making them faster and more efficient.

Confidence was waning in regards to building vessels for the British market, and the collapse of James Duncan and Company in 1878, along with the failure of the Bank of Prince Edward Island three years later, did nothing to instill confidence in local shipbuilders.

However, Peake Brothers and Company continued to move forward. As demand permitted, the firm had vessels built for sale abroad, as well as for their own fleet. Many of these vessels were built at Mount Stewart, where the company owned property; it was now one of the main shipbuilding sites on Prince Edward Island. In addition, the brothers continued to expand the Peake waterfront holdings in Charlottetown by adding a third wharf, at the foot of Great George Street in 1872.

Following their marriage, James and his wife, Edith, lived in his father's old house on Water Street, but the young man had higher ambitions. In 1876, William C. Harris, a brilliant Charlottetown architect, was commissioned to design a truly extravagant mansion for the family.

The result was an ornate twenty-five-room home complete with marble fireplaces and the most modern conveniences, such as central heating and hot and cold running water. Located on Kent Street overlooking the harbour, the house was estimated to cost $50,000, an immense sum at the time. James named the place Beaconsfield in memory of his idol, Benjamin Disraeli, Britain's Prime Minister, who became the Earl of Beaconsfield.

The Peakes had barely settled at Beaconsfield when an international depression struck Island shipbuilding heavily. Furthermore, in 1879, Ralph—perhaps the smartest of the three brothers—died at the age of thirty-four. A month later, Alice also passed away; within weeks, the family had lost two of its most capable members.

In spite of the bleak economic conditions, James continued to live extravagantly. He was forced to borrow money extensively, using his

James Peake Jr., whose great ambition and extravagant lifestyle were destroyed by the economic depression of 1879.

house and his one-third share of the business as collateral. In 1881, the Bank of Prince Edward Island failed, and James Jr.'s debts increased by some $10,000 for his liability as a director and shareholder. The following year, heavily in debt and unable to obtain any more credit, James signed over his share in the business to his partners and retired. He and Edith were forced to witness their Beaconsfield belongings being auctioned off. The couple moved to a much smaller home, owned by Edith's father, but a few years later James moved out and for a time lived elsewhere in Charlottetown. In the late 1880s, he travelled to Minnesota and found work as a bookkeeper before moving to Victoria, British Columbia, where he became a liquor merchant. He lost that business and on July 7, 1895, James died in abject poverty; his riches-to-rags saga was over.

In 1890, Peake Brothers and Company folded. The company's last vessel, the brigantine *Zenith*, was launched that year by David Egan at Mount Stewart. It was sold to a Norwegian buyer four years later, and thus completed the Peake years of shipbuilding.

James Jr.'s elegant Beaconsfield is now the headquarters of the Prince Edward Island Museum and Heritage Foundation. Peake's Quay—a vibrant variety of shops and restaurants—stands on the site of the original Peake waterfront holdings.

The final chapter in the story of Prince Edward Island

The handsome little brig Zinga, *built at Mount Stewart in 1877 and co-owned by the Peake brothers and Thomas Handrahan. Like many vessels of the period it met a violent end, wrecked on Cape Porcupine, Canso Gut, in the winter of 1882.*

Designed by prominent architect William Critchlow Harris, James Peake Jr.'s home Beaconsfield was a Second Empire mansion combining opulent display with the most modern conveniences.

Stripped of some its Victorian fripperies, Beaconsfield remains a prominent feature of the Charlottetown streetscape. Today it houses the offices of the Prince Edward Island Museum and Heritage Foundation, and its rooms are restored in the period style.

Shipyard near Murray Harbour, P.E.I., about 1870. The scene is typical of yards throughout the region, where the requirements for building were simple: a sloped site close to deep water, a blacksmith shop, housing for workers, and ready access to local timber.

commercial sailing ships began in the mid-1870s, when the days of the square-rigger were nearing an end but there was still a place for the three-masted schooners or terns. These vessels carried a worthwhile cargo, required a relatively small crew and entered small harbours that were inaccessible to larger vessels.

In all, thirteen of these vessels were built on Prince Edward Island. Among the first were the *Bride, Bridegroom* and *Bridesmaid*, all built in Bideford between 1874 and 1876 for S. Hoskins and Co. of Swansea, Wales. The first two were employed in the coal and copper-ore trade between Wales and Chile, a trade that required well-made vessels to carry the heavy cargos around Cape Horn. The *Bridesmaid* was sold to Norway and disappeared in 1902.

One of the last, the *Victory Chimes*, was launched at Cardigan in 1918 and was well known around Bay of Fundy ports for many years. The last was the *Anna MacDonald*, and when it was launched also in Cardigan in 1920, the chapter of building cargo-carrying sailing vessels on Prince Edward Island came to a close.

Chapter Three

NEWPORT LANDING
AND AVONDALE SHIPBUILDERS

Late in the evening of February 5, 1883, the barque *Hannah Blanchard* labours westward across the North Atlantic through heavy seas and near gale-force winds. It is a black night, without a star in sight, and the only sound is the wind whistling through the rigging and the crash of the sea against the vessel's hull.

Captain J.S. Williams is keeping the deck, as he has done almost continuously since leaving Falmouth, England. He has two worries: the weather and his extremely sick wife lying below in their stateroom. Some of the watch can dimly see the captain pacing the deck. Suddenly the *Hannah Blanchard* is struck by a mountainous wave that sweeps the vessel from stem to stern. When the seamen look aft again, there is no sign of the captain. A search ensues but there is only one possibility: Captain Williams was washed overboard. Close relatives would later conclude that because of fatigue and personal worries the captain failed to notice the sea that claimed him.

The *Hannah Blanchard* was built by James Mosher at Newport Landing in 1878. For over eighty years Mosher, with associated relatives including John A. Harvie and George and William Mounce, built more than 160 sailing vessels, all big enough to sail the oceans of the world. This small hamlet that was such a force in shipbuilding is illustrative of the many small communities that produced large numbers of wooden sailing vessels along the coasts of the Maritime provinces.

The story of Newport Landing goes back at least to the seventeenth century. The remains of several buildings in the immediate area suggest that a small Acadian settlement almost certainly existed. When the French-speaking inhabitants were forcibly removed from Nova Scotia, great areas of cleared land opened up that Governor Charles Lawrence thought would accommodate some 20,000 families, many hailing from New England. On October 12, 1758, and again on January 11, 1759, he issued proclamations offering these vacated lands to settlers, specifying 100 acres of land per head of family with fifty additional acres for each additional family member. He also stipulated that a "quit-rent" of one shilling sterling per annum be paid for every fifty acres, but the Quit-Rents would not commence for ten years after the date of the grant. Grantees would be obliged to plant, cultivate or improve one-third of their land within ten years, another third within twenty years and the final third within thirty years. The proclamation went on to state that the lands being offered had been cultivated for more than 100 years, had never produced failed crops or needed manure.

It was an attractive invitation, and after agents from New

Looking west along the Avon River from Fort Edward in the mid-eighteenth century. In the foreground colonial sloops take advantage of the rising tide. Beyond, across the mouth of the St. Croix River, are the sloping banks of Newport Landing.

England had examined and approved the lands the settlers began to arrive. The so-called New England Planters, a term synonymous with colonists, found the offer quite tempting. Among the 8000 Planters who came to Nova Scotia, there were 13 families totalling 58 people that arrived at Newport Landing from Newport, Rhode Island, on the sloops *Lydia* and *Sally*. These new settlers were mostly farmers, with a few merchants and skilled artisans.

One of the early arrivals was James Mosher, with his wife Lydia

View of the Avon River from Retreat Farm, Windsor, in 1840. This pastoral scene with livestock in the foreground and shipping in the river beyond is characteristic of the region, where farming and shipbuilding grew up side by side.

Mosher." It had a capacity of about 60 tons and was built by James Mosher's son Nicholas.

Whether Acadians built any vessels in the area is open to conjecture. They definitely built small fishing vessels in other parts of Nova Scotia, primarily as a sideline to farming. It is possible that one small vessel was built in the Newport Landing area by a shipwright named Neal McCurdy, after the arrival of the Planters, but historians generally credit Nicholas Mosher's sloop as the first.

Mosher also put his engineering skills to work when he constructed a bridge over the Avon River in 1795, for which he received £837 in payment. The bridge and their four children; eight more were born in their new home. The first vessel of any size to be built in Newport Landing was a sloop, launched in 1807. An 1891 history of the Mosher family states that it "was sloop-rigged and was sailed for a time by Captain Barzillai was used constantly until 1816. By the end of 1796, he had also built bridges over the nearby Cogmagun and Kennetcook rivers.

The most active shipbuilders in the Mosher family descended from two of Nicholas's brothers, Jehu and George. Jehu and his wife,

A view from the prosperous town of Windsor in 1842 looking downriver towards Newport Landing. Small coasting vessels crowd the stream along with an early steamship, distinguished from her sisters only by a proud plume of coal smoke drifting towards Falmouth on the river's north bank.

A modern reconstruction of the arrival of New England settlers at Newport Landing in the 1760s. Some of these settlers travelled to Nova Scotia in their own ships, and many possessed the skills of both the farmer and the mariner, skills they would put to good use in their new homes. The sloops Lydia *and* Sally, *on the right side of the painting, brought fifty-eight settlers to this site.*

The ship Lansdowne, *gaily festooned on the launching ways at the J.B. North shipyard in Hantsport. On the left, amid the usual clutter of an active yard, is the tidal-powered block mill of Rathbun and Company, which used the immense tidal range of the Avon River to help rig vessels built throughout the estuary.*

Hannah, produced two sons: Jehu Jr., who fathered Silas, and Nicholas (known as Nicholas Sr.), who later worked with his son James and his grandson Thomas. George and his wife, Margaret, produced sons Ira and Nicholas (known as Nicholas, Jr.) and a daughter who married Elkanah Harvie. Their son, John Andrew Harvie, was a prominent builder with the Moshers. Another

daughter married Richard Mounce, and their sons William and Captain George became very involved with the family shipping business. Finally, William Henry, son of Silas, was one of the last of the shipbuilding Moshers.

Exactly when the first Mosher shipyard was established is not certain; it may have been when Nicholas Sr. built the *Two Sisters* in

Top: A schooner framed up and ready for planking. The gently sloping beaches of the Minas Basin were ideal for wooden shipbuilding, with predictable high tides making launches considerably less risky than elsewhere.

Bottom right: Builder's crew at Cox Shipyard, Kingsport, pose alongside the nearly-completed hull of their latest project. Some carry the tools of their various trades—T-squares, augers, caulker's mallets—while at right a teamster manages his horses, who wait patiently just out of frame.

Top: Two workers hang a plank on the turn of the bilge of a vessel under construction.

Bottom left: Shipyard crew poses with their tools in front of a schooner under construction at Newport Landing, around 1880. Two are shouldering ship's knees, strong, naturally curved timbers used to support a vessel's deck.

Bottom right: Nearly obscured by a clutter of unsawn timber and staging, a vessel in the early stages of framing up begins to take its distinctive wishbone shape.

Builders of wooden ships achieved a high degree of craftsmanship with a few relatively simple tools. Clockwise from upper left: shipwright's broadaxe and adze, the former used to impart remarkably subtle bevels to squared timbers, the latter to cut notches across a timber's grain; a pin maul, used to drive wooden fasteners; a hardwood caulking mallet, used with a chisel-shaped iron to drive oakum caulking between a vessel's planks; an auger used to make holes to receive treenails and iron bolts; a plane for smoothing the rough edges of planks.

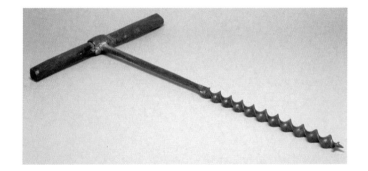

Wooden shipbuilding required the cooperation of a variety of skilled craftsmen. Clockwise from left: a labourer wields a heavy mallet for driving treenails; a carpenter braces an auger against his chest, driving holes for fasteners; a caulker wields his mallet and iron to force oakum into deck seams.

Portrait of Capt. George Mounce. (Artist: David MacIntosh)

The J.B. King wharf, Avondale, at low tide. Because of the Minas Basin's immense tidal range, wharves were often monumental timber structures extending far into the water in order to accommodate large vessels at high tide.

1829. The other Mosher yard that sprang up alongside was run by John A. Harvie and William H. Mosher, who launched their brig *Caledonia* in 1839 followed by the brig *Flora MacDonald* in 1840.

The Mosher yards were typical of shipbuilding sites all over the region, and the building of the vessels began with a half model carved to scale that incorporated the desired features, which served as the blueprint. The keel, the backbone of the vessel, was a massive timber measuring approximately twenty-four by fourteen inches for a medium-sized vessel. To the keel were fastened the skeletal parts—the stem, sternpost and frames or ribs. When these were in place, heavy keelsons were fastened over the keel to strengthen the vessel even more.

At this point, an inner skin of planking was fastened to the inside frames to add strength to the frame and protect it from cargos. Then came the outside planking; for a 1200-ton vessel, 200 feet in length, the planking next to the keel would be eight inches thick on the lowest parts of the hull, but only about five inches thick

A modern painting of the Mosher Shipyard, Avondale, showing the Regent *nearing completion on the ways. The artist's perspective is accurate: the vessels often towered over the quite modest communities that built them. (Artist: David MacIntosh)*

The three-masted barque John A. Harvie *taking in sail as she proceeds smartly, close to Cape Blomidon: the skysails are furled, the foreroyal loose. (Artist: David MacIntosh)*

watertight. With caulking irons and mallets, they forced oakum into the seams before paying them over with hot pitch. While the planking was in process, the decks would be laid and caulked, the cabin and fo'c'sle completed and the rudder hung. Other equipment such as windlass, winch and anchors would be put in place and the vessel painted.

Most vessels were launched with only their lower masts installed; they would be towed to a nearby port to have their masts and rigging completed. Others were launched fully rigged and ready for sea.

During summer and winter, the working day began at sunrise and ended at sunset. In 1853, shipbuilder Joseph Salter of Moncton agreed to a ten-hour day; he was perhaps the first to do so in the Maritimes.

Shipyard workers' wages varied over time. In the 1840s, shipwrights could be hired for £50 per year, but a dollar per day, and a little more for specialists such as caulkers and riggers was more common. In a few instances, workmen took out a share or two in a vessel in lieu of wages. This way they would receive a share in the profits so long as the ship was afloat.

The Moshers arrived on the shipbuilding scene at a good time. Nova Scotia's Lieutenant-Governor John G. LeMarchant was proud to report: "In 1846 Nova Scotia owned 2503 vessels; Canada but 604; New Brunswick but 730; Newfoundland but 937; Prince Edward Island 265. The tonnage of

higher up the hull. Only a steam box could soften planks of this thickness prior to changing their conformation to the curved shapes that formed the hull.

Once the vessel was planked, the caulkers made the ship

Construction of the Parthena, *with Capt. George Mounce in a frock coat and builder J.A. Harvie. The barrels on the roof are filled with water, at the ready for a possible fire (Artist: David MacIntosh).*

The tidy-looking barque J.E. Graham, *built at Avondale in 1881, alongside at an unidentified European port.*

all these colonies collectively was, in that year, 252,832 tons, while that of Nova Scotia alone reached as high as 141,093 tons." He went on to state, "that Nova Scotia is destined, at no distant day, to be one of the largest shipowning countries in the world is apparent from the status already achieved."

In 1847 the yard operated by Nicholas Jr., Ira and Silas launched the *Jenny Lind*, which was recognized as the first full-rigged ship built in Hants County. After the launching, Ira took it to Saint John to load. At the time, there was a typhus epidemic in the city. Tragically, Ira was struck down by the disease and died on January 4, 1848, leaving Silas and Nicholas Jr. to manage the shipyard. Nicholas became the master builder and in the early 1860s they were joined by his nephew, John Andrew Harvie, first as a master builder then later as a full-fledged partner. At some point, Nicholas Jr. sold or otherwise disposed of his share of the shipyard to Harvie, although he continued to turn out vessels in the same yard until the early 1880s.

The three-masted ship Regent, *built by J.A. Harvie at Avondale in 1878, under tow in constricted waters. Her crew, lined up along the rail aft, seem to be looking out diligently for the bottom.*

When Silas Mosher died in 1865, his son William H. Mosher took over, stating, "My share being one-half of the shipyard now occupied by John A. Harvie together with one-half of the buildings." For years the yard was known as the Mosher-Harvie shipyard. John A. Harvie died in 1882, and William H. Mosher became the sole owner; it was he who closed out the yard following the launch of the ship *Angola* in 1890.

In his time Nicholas Jr. produced more than twenty-three vessels, ranging in size from the 100-ton schooner *Neva* to the 1529-ton *Tuskar*. The schooner was lost on the Labrador coast in 1869, and the *Tuskar* was sold to an Italian buyer in 1899 for $20,750. John A. Harvie launched twenty-one vessels ranging in size from the 368-ton barquentine *Richard Pearse* to the 1336-ton barque *J.E. Graham*. William

The famous ship William D. Lawrence, *launched at Maitland, N.S. in October of 1874. At a length of 262 feet and with a displacement of 2458 tons, she was the largest sailing ship ever built in the Maritime provinces.*

H. Mosher is credited with launching five vessels late in the yard's history. His smallest was the three-masted schooner *Severn* launched in 1884, and his largest and last was the 1551-ton *Angola*. In total, the yard launched at least forty-nine registered vessels.

In the adjoining shipyard, Nicholas Mosher Sr. launched twenty-five known vessels from 1829 until his death in 1871. His smallest was

A charming portrait of the Maitland barque Launberga.

the brig *Curlew* at 141 tons, launched in 1839, and the largest was the 934-ton ship *Virginia*, completed in 1862. His son contributed another seventeen vessels, including the large ship *Record* at 1691 tons. Nicholas Sr.'s grandson Thomas, the last relative to operate in this shipyard, built eighteen vessels. The largest constructed by any of the Moshers was his ship *J.D. Everett* at 1957 tons, launched in 1889. The last vessel built by Thomas, and the last built in Nicholas Sr.'s shipyard, was the barquentine *Avola*, launched in 1892. When the *Avola* took to the water, the Moshers' shipbuilding enterprise in Newport Landing came to an end. In total, this shipyard added at least sixty vessels to the Mosher output.

Other Moshers related to the aforementioned shipbuilders contributed five more vessels to the Moshers' roster but it is not known if they were built in one of these yards or elsewhere. It is, however, safe to assume that Mosher-built vessels totalled at least 114. If the forty-nine registered vessels built by others are added, there were at least 163 sailing vessels that came from Newport Landing, all measuring forty tons or more.

Although the Moshers operated two shipyards, there were frequent interchanges when it came to financing the vessels. For instance, when Nicholas Sr. built the barque *Ava* in 1855, Nicholas Jr.,

from the other yard, was one of the shareholders. Conversely, when Nicholas Jr. built the barque *Venus* in 1869, both Nicholas Sr. and his son James were among the shareholders.

It was a sign of the times that when Nicholas Mosher Sr. died in 1871, he owned 18 shares in the ship *N. Mosher*, 16 shares in the ship *Nancy M.*, 10 shares in the barque *Venus* and 8 shares in the ship *Iris*. When William Henry Mosher died in 1903, he didn't own a share in any vessel.

The Mounce family was closely connected to the Moshers, especially by marriage. William Mounce, who was listed as a shipwright, owned shares in at least fourteen vessels that came from Mosher yards. His brother, George, went to sea early in life, rose to command and became an agent for the ship brokerage firm of Andrew Gibson and Company in Liverpool, England. The Gibson firm owned shares in several Mosher vessels, including the three barquentines *St. Croix*, *St. Paul* and *St. Peter*. Captain George Mounce was the sole owner of six vessels built in the Mosher yards, including the "R" ships— *Regent*, *Rialto* and *Record*. The latter, at 1691 tons, was the second largest of all the Mosher vessels. In addition, Captain Mounce was the sole owner of the ship *Mohur*, which was built by Joseph Monteith in his Maitland shipyard in 1874. Mounce also owned some shares in other Mosher vessels and may have been part owner of vessels built elsewhere.

In his "Notes On Shipbuilding In Newport Landing," L.S. Loomer lists some of the daily wages paid to shipyard workers in nearby Windsor in 1873. They include: shipwrights, $2.00-$2.50; cabinetmakers, $2.00; and carpenters, $2.00. These wages did not include room and board, which cost about $3.50 per week.

Dwarfed by his creation, a shipcarver admires the eponymous figurehead he has fashioned for the great ship William D. Lawrence.

The three-masted ship Forest King, *built by J.B. North at Hantsport in 1877. It was remarkably long-lived for a wooden sailing ship, serving for 22 years in the North fleet before being transferred to Italian ownership in 1899 and finally being converted into a hulk in 1913.*

The costs involved in construction of a vessel were quite substantial. If the builder was working under contract to the owner, a formal agreement was drawn up specifying the vessel's dimensions, the types of wood to be used in the various parts of the ship, the choice of fastenings, the cabins and the stepping of the masts. All of the construction, from the figurehead to the crow's nest, from the stem to the stern, were accounted for. The owner agreed to pay the builder a set amount, say $25 per registered ton, and the payments were made according to a schedule, sometimes monthly, sometimes when the vessel reached certain stages of construction. A sum was always held back until the vessel was launched, the builder's certificate was turned over and the owner was satisfied with the final result.

The investment was large. In Windsor, in 1863, a ship of 934 tons cost $37,300, and in Maitland, a decade later, a barque of 1100 tons was valued at $50,000. For the 1647-ton ship *George T. Hay* launched at Spencers Island in 1887, timber, iron and outfitting each cost about $12,000, while labour was charged at $21,000. The return on this investment had to come fairly quickly as records indicate that many vessels were lost within a few years of being launched.

The museum situated on the site of the two Mosher shipyards is dedicated to preserving the story of the New England Planters, as well as the history of local shipbuilding, and it is also helping preserve the

The Avon River Heritage Society Museum in Avondale, established to interpret the maritime history of the Avon River region. In recent years the society launched the Avon Spirit, *a replica of a traditional coastal schooner. The museum is built on the site of the Mosher shipyards.*

skills of building wooden boats. The Avon Spirit Shipyard, which was established to build the 35-ton replica of the *Avon Spirit* in 1997, offers courses in building small wooden craft. The quiet village of Avondale is a far cry today from the waterfronts of such cities as Saint John and Charlottetown. A few handsome Mounce mansions are the most visible legacy of the Mosher and Mounce enterprises that turned a Planter Settlement into a busy shipbuilding centre.

Chapter Four

THE KILLAM FLEET

The earliest known landing by Europeans in south-west Nova Scotia was made by Samuel de Champlain and company in 1604. They entered present-day Yarmouth harbour past a landmark they called Cape Forchu (forked cape). In 1651, Charles La Tour brought a group of French colonists to the area, and that same year Sieur Mieus d'Entremont and his family landed at Pubnico. This was the beginning of French attempts at settlement in the region.

The first English-speaking settlers arrived from New England in 1761, after France had been forced to cede power to Britain. The group included men such as Moses Perry, Sealed Landers, Ebenezer Ellis and their families. Settlement began at Chebogue near the mouth of Yarmouth harbour, but as more New Englanders arrived they moved further north toward the present town site.

These early settlers, and those that followed, were enticed by

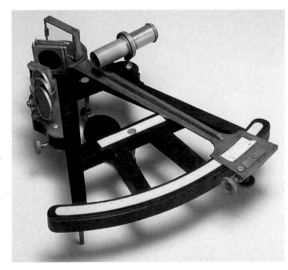

Sextant used to take bearings at sea from the sun, and maintain the designated course.

promises of free land. They were quite possibly sensing the first seeds of unrest that, in a few short years, would take root and grow into revolution. They came primarily as farmers, but upon finding that much of the land was not suitable for agriculture, they turned to the sea, for fishing. This gave birth to coastal trade both locally and as far south as the West Indies. Small vessels left Yarmouth loaded with timber and salt fish and returned with manufactured goods, as well as sugar, molasses, salt and rum—from such places as Boston and the West Indies.

By 1879, these trades and the demand for more vessels spawned a shipbuilding and shipowning industry that placed Yarmouth among the leading shipowning ports in Canada. Like other Maritime shipbuilding centres, there was an abundant supply of raw materials to build vessels and to supply cargos. Indeed, production was so great that

A romantic view of the young township of Yarmouth in the early nineteenth century. Already the harbour bustles with activity: in the foreground, a shapely skiff pulls for a coastal schooner; in the background, beyond the town, a brig lies at anchor.

View north along Yarmouth's Main Street, 1829. Along the town's raw waterfront lies a merchant brig with painted gunports behind which another merchantman, her masts unstepped, undergoes repair at a primitive shipyard.

Yarmouth developed its own specialists: shipwrights, caulkers, riggers, sail-makers and blacksmiths.

Yarmouth's shipping industry began in the late eighteenth century, expanding gradually to burst into full flower in the 1860s and 1870s. Among the earliest recorded vessels built in Yarmouth was the small schooner *Janet*, launched by John H. Killam and Josiah Porter in 1788. During the twenty-year period from 1830 to the mid-1850s, the Killam involvement in shipping grew rapidly. In the 1830s they only had interests in seven vessels; over the next two decades thirty-six more were added to their holdings. By 1879 Yarmouth Township could claim ownership of 297 vessels that were known on every ocean. For instance, in that same year on one June weekend alone reports announced the safe arrivals of 29 Yarmouth vessels in

different ports around the world. Unlike some other Maritime entrepreneurs, the Yarmouth builders were not building their vessels for overseas owners; they were both shipbuilders and shipowners.

From the launch of the *Janet* until the loss of John H. Killam's schooner *Grace Rice* in 1899, the Killams owned wholly or partially at least 105 vessels. During the halcyon days of the 1860s and 1870s the family contributed upwards of fifty vessels to Yarmouth's fleets.

These boom years were the result of several factors. First, the American Civil War had decimated U.S. fleets and there was an urgent need for bottoms (the contemporary term for vessels). Second, traditional shipbuilding skills were now well established in the community, as was the business of overseas trading. Third, the raw materials needed to build the vessels and provide cargos were still readily available. It is worth noting that although steamships were beginning to come into use at this time, they were not yet a serious competitor to Maritime sailing vessels.

In the 1860s and 1870s, Yarmouth builders began to produce large vessels—barques and full-rigged ships—to service the developing foreign trade. Thomas Killam led the way when, in 1861, he launched the 1460-ton ship *Research*, which was the largest vessel built in the township to that date.

The first John Killam, the builder of the *Janet*, arrived in Yarmouth from Wenham, Massachusetts, in 1776. His

A tern schooner, small coasters and yachts drift past a barque tied up along the Yarmouth waterfront in the late nineteenth century. In the background looms the elaborate bulk of the Grand Hotel. (Artist: Jennie Morrow)

Thomas Killam Sr., pioneer Yarmouth shipbuilder and merchant.

son, John the younger, established a shipyard that was central to the Killams' business activities; from there they launched numerous vessels. However, they also had vessels built for them in many different places in the surrounding counties, as well as across the Bay of Fundy in New Brunswick. And, they acquired either sole ownership or shares in vessels first constructed for others.

While the senior and junior John Killams began the family business, it was John Jr.'s sons—Thomas, Samuel and Benjamin—who

moved the business to the forefront of Yarmouth's shipping and commercial endeavours and prepared the fourth generation—a total of six brothers and cousins—to continue at the helm. The Killams were by no means the only family to develop Yarmouth County shipping. Master builders during the mid-nineteenth century included Nathaniel, Nelson and Freeman Gardner, John and Henry Richards, Dennis Horton, Denis Surette, Benjamin Rogers, John Vickery, Robert Sims and Frederick Weston. Further up the Bay of Fundy, the Raymonds, Jenkins and Crosby, as well as Spencer, Richards and Company also contributed vessels to the Yarmouth fleets.

The men who invested in these vessels represented the backbone of Yarmouth township's economy. Prominent names in

A postcard view capturing the variety of Yarmouth's port traffic at the height of the age of sail: a small coastal steamer, a slab-sided tern schooner, an iron-hulled barque, and full-rigged ships drying sail.

fishery, including the firm of Kinney and Corning, as well as Moody, Brown Company.

Like any town of this size, there were doctors—the Yarmouth Medical Society was formed in 1867. There were also dentists, druggists, an undertaker, tailors, grocers and jewellers. The commercial manufacture of boots, shoes, carriages and furniture was also in evidence. In 1839, the Bank of Nova Scotia established a branch in Yarmouth, followed by the Bank of Yarmouth in 1865 and the Exchange Bank in 1869.

As the shipping industry expanded, it was inevitable that improvements would be made to navigation within the harbour. The Cape Forchu light was lit for the first time on January 15, 1840. In 1848, markers donated by Thomas Killam were placed along the west

the heyday of shipping included Robbins, Stoneman, Goudey, Brown, Moody, Lovitt, Law, Cann, Doane, Dennis, Churchill, Baker, Clements and Perry.

Naturally, the town and its maritime industries grew along parallel lines. In 1864–65 the *Yarmouth Herald* reported that there were 558 dwellings, 50 retail shops, 30 wharves, 7 churches, 2 iron foundries and 3 fire houses in the town. Children who attended the three primary schools might go on to the Yarmouth Academy, a secondary school that was replaced in 1864 by the Yarmouth Seminary.

The town of Yarmouth was a bustling commercial centre with many businesses related to shipping. Sailmakers included the Weddletons, Zebina Goudey and Adams and Turner. The Burrell and Johnson Iron Foundry, blockmakers William Currier and Son, and many blacksmiths all provided services to the shipyards. Small-boat builders such as W. and J. Crawley and ship chandlers were all founded to fill a need. Numerous businesses provided supplies to the

The headquarters of the Killam Brothers' shipowning and mercantile establishment, a landmark on the Yarmouth waterfront since the mid-1830s. Today it houses a museum interpreting the town's rich shipping history.

Crowds throng busy Brown's wharf on the town's waterfront, while in the background lie paddle- and screw steamers of the Yarmouth Steamship Company. By the late nineteenth century Yarmouth was a busy industrial centre with regular passenger links to cities on the eastern seaboard.

side of the channel. The harbour's beacon light began operating on February 16, 1874.

For many decades, Yarmouth harbour was filled with masts—vessels moored to wharves or anchored in the harbour, with others constantly departing and arriving. During this period many Yarmouth-built and Yarmouth-owned vessels never saw their home port. They travelled all over the globe, transporting oil from New York and Philadelphia to ports in the British Isles, Europe and the Far East.

Cargos of grain, pitch pine, cotton and mahogany, along with guano from the west coast of South America, all had to be shipped across the Atlantic. As the wooden square-riggers aged, insurance standards limited the type of insurable cargos they could carry. Many an old windship ended its working days freighting unsinkable lumber, with a windmill pump working continuously to keep the leakage in check.

The cargos these vessels brought back to the Americas from Europe included iron rails, pumice stone, empty oil barrels, marble,

Workers pose in front of the Gridley blacksmith shop on Water Street. This was one of many businesses providing custom ironwork for the town's immense volume of shipping.

1872. Almost immediately the vessel was caught in a terrible winter storm; rain and sleet swept the vessel, reducing visibility to near zero, and gale-force winds drove it off course. In the black of the second night at sea, the vessel struck a shoal near Penzance, England. The captain attempted to carry a rope ashore with his young son in his arms, but the boy was swept from his father and never seen again. A heavy sea smashed the pilot house in which the captain's wife and baby daughter had sought refuge; both of them drowned. One sailor also drowned, but the rest of the officers and crew managed to reach shore safely.

While such losses were frequent, many other vessels were saved by the dogged and skilful perseverance of their officers and crew. On November 10, 1866, Thomas Killam's ship *Research* departed Quebec for Scotland with a load of timber. On November 23, when it was well out in the Atlantic, the ship was struck by a sudden winter storm. Sails were shredded and an enormous wave broke the rudder-stock

soda ash, glass, bleaching powder and other manufactured goods. Cargos brought back from ports in the Far East often included sugar, wool and straw braid.

Over the years, Yarmouth deservedly earned a place among the foremost shipbuilding and ship-owning centres in Canada. Shipping registers and the records compiled by the late J. Murray Lawson, the town's contemporary historian of local shipping, reveal that some 2100 vessels were owned in Yarmouth County during the nineteenth century. But the losses were heavy; 823 known vessels were lost in that period, including more than 70 that disappeared with everyone on board. There were few Yarmouth families who could not count close relatives—men women and children—among those lost at sea.

The Yarmouth barque *Manitobah*, under the command of Captain A.R. Durkee, departed Le Havre, France, on January 30,

Interior of the Parker-Eakins sail loft, where experienced sailmakers work with needle, palm, and fid to shape the acres of canvas required for a square-rigged merchant vessel.

and snapped the rudder chains. The *Research* was sailing out of control.

To save the ship, someone had to go over the stern with tackles and attempt to harness the flailing rudder. The mate, young Aaron Flint Churchill, stripped bare and with one hand holding the tackle—the other kept free to keep him from being pounded against the hull—he went over the stern in a double bowline. After spending ninety minutes in the freezing water, he managed to hook the tackle into the rudder's ringbolt. Hauled back on deck nearly unconscious, Churchill was revived only to climb out again with the second tackle. He was successful again but this time it took even longer to accomplish. In the end, it was all for nothing; the next day the seas tore the rudder away. But Captain George W. Churchill refused to give up. Time and again jury rudders were rigged, only to be broken or swept away. The battered hull began to leak and the *Research* was driven far off course. The eighth rudder held, and eighty-eight days after leaving Quebec the indomitable Captain Churchill brought his ship into Greenock, Scotland.

Aaron Churchill went on to command other vessels, but while he was still in his twenties he left the sea and moved to Savannah, Georgia, where he established a stevedoring business and, later, the Churchill line of steamships. He never forgot his roots, and in 1889 he built a large summer home at Darling's Lake, which he named "The Anchorage." He spent his summers there until his death in 1920.

Yarmouth's business and cultural life developed with a great deal of input and help from the Killams. In 1839, Thomas Killam constructed the Rialto, a large building that housed a machine shop, a

The smokestacks of the Burrill-Johnson Iron Company in Yarmouth are signs of productivity and success in this advertising bulletin. Iron foundries were essential in providing fastenings and other metalwork for wooden sailing vessels.

carding mill, a planing machine and a block shop. In 1863, when the Yarmouth Gas Light Company was inaugurated, Samuel Killam Sr. became its president. The Western Counties Railway was incorporated in 1870; Frank Killam was one of its directors. Rail service began operating to Digby in 1879, and connections were established to Halifax in 1891. Samuel Killam Jr. was a director of the Yarmouth Skating Club when it opened in 1878. When the Yarmouth Duck and Yarn Company, later the Cosmos Cotton

Shipping and mercantile activity brought great prosperity to Yarmouth in the late nineteenth century, changing the face of the town. At top, the Phoenix Rink, a monumental timber-frame structure that housed industrial and agricultural exhibitions until it was destroyed by fire in 1893. Bottom left, a view of Main Street showing the substantial premises of McLaughlin Brothers, retailers of European luxury goods, silverware, jewelry, and imported groceries. Bottom right, the Grand Hotel decked with flags and bunting to celebrate the visit of Governor General Lord Aberdeen.

Prosperity brought a refined social and cultural life to the town. At top, a view of the affluent residential area of Forest Street showing the homes of shipowner George Cann Lewis, master mariner Captain John E. Murphy, and businessman Asa Ellsworth McGray, manager with the Yarmouth Steamship Company. Bottom left, gaily dressed children play croquet and cricket on the lawn of Yarmouth Seminary, an institution endowed by George Killam to educate the youth of the town. Bottom right, the humble keeper's house at Cape Forchu light, as important to Yarmouth's fortunes as the mansions that lined the town's finest residential streets.

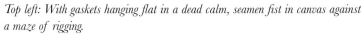

Top left: With gaskets hanging flat in a dead calm, seamen fist in canvas against a maze of rigging.
Bottom left: The Samuel Killam-owned ship N. & E. Gardner *at Chincha Island, Peru, a centre of the unglamorous but highly profitable guano trade. At her launch in 1864 it was the largest vessel ever built by Yarmouth concerns; she was lost in the Atlantic in 1878 after a month-long battle with unrelenting gales.*
Below: An experienced hand at the huge wheel of the four-masted barque Iranian *in heavy weather in the Pacific.*

Above: The engine of a sailing ship: a section of the acres of canvas and miles of rigging that drove a merchant vessel across the oceans of the world.

Top right: Iranian *looking forlorn under bare poles against smokestacks and gasworks at Bayonne, New Jersey: in port, the glamour of the sailing ship was eclipsed by the practical needs of commerce.*

Bottom right: Working among the organised clutter of the poop deck, crew members of the Iranian *bend on a new sail while en route to Japan.*

The barque Lima in a perilous state with its headsails blown out and bowsprit gone. It is in imminent danger of dismasting. In the background another vessel stands by to render assistance.

insurance to cover vessels and cargo was of paramount importance. The first step was taken in 1809 when the Marine Insurance Company of Yarmouth was formed. John Killam Jr. was a director before it closed in 1812, at the beginning of the war. Over the next several decades, the Yarmouth Marine Insurance Company (1837), the Acadian Insurance Company (1858), the Commercial Insurance Company (1861) and the Atlantic Insurance Company (1865) were formed, each with one or more Killams among the shareholders. Two additional local insurance companies followed in the early 1870s, the Pacific and the Oriental. All of the companies were financially successful and all were backed by local entrepreneurs. However, all of them shut their doors in the 1880s with the decline of sailing vessels out of Yarmouth.

Company, was created in 1883, Samuel Killam Jr. was its vice-president, Thomas, Jr. was the secretary-treasurer and Frank Killam was a director.

From the earliest days of shipping in Yarmouth, the need for

Thomas Killam Sr. had a long association with politics. First elected to the Nova Scotia legislature in 1847, he won re-election in three succeeding provincial elections. An outspoken opponent of Confederation, he came to accept the inevitable, and in the federal election of September of 1867 he won a resounding

With her sharp bow and dramatically raked masts, the three-masted barque A.J. Fulton *in this fine portrait embodies the speed and romance of the age of merchant sail at its height.*

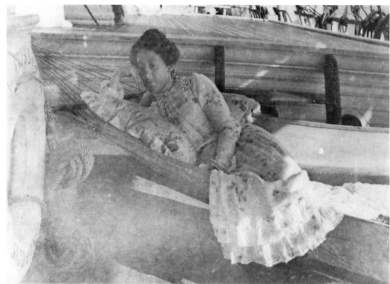

Below: Abyssinia*'s cabin was furnished with all the requisites of a Victorian parlour ashore including, at left, a reed organ, providing a comforting familiarity whether in Marseilles, Yokohama, or Callao.*

Young Marion Hilton courts the attention of Abyssinia*'s proud mascot Fiddle (bottom left) while underway in warm lattitudes, and (centre) takes a look at her surroundings through the binocilars.*

Merchant sailing ships were homes as well as workplaces. As the nineteenth century progressed it became increasingly common for families to accompany master mariners on passages to all the oceans of the world. On board the barque Abyssinia*, Cora Hilton (left), wife of master Arthur W. Hilton, takes advantage of a calm to relax in a hammock rigged on the poopdeck.*

*Even the roughest foremast hands have turned out in their finest
clothes for a christening ceremony on board the newly-launched ship*
Alexander Yeats *(above), in 1876.*

*Elaborately-hatted visitors (centre) pay their respects to Cora and
Marion Hilton on board* Abyssinia *during a port visit.*

*Comfortable in bare feet and shirtsleeves, Captain Isaac Webster (left) of the
barque* Iranian *uses a sextant to take a sight at midday.*

Above: The home of Aaron "Rudder" Churchill outside Yarmouth, viewed from the water.
Top left: The former Killam Brothers mercantile establishment on the Yarmouth waterfront, now maintained as a museum.
Far left: The Pelton-Fuller House, legacy of the town's shipping golden age, and now home of the Yarmouth County Historical Society.
Above: Dedicatory plaque from the sextant presented to Aaron Churchill in recognition of his heroic efforts to save the ship Research.

Above: The classical symmetry of Yarmouth Academy, one of the township's oldest cultural institutions.

Right: One of the many surviving Victorian mansions in Yarmouth testifying to the town's nineteenth-century mercantile strength.

The ship Research, *George W. Churchill master. In November of 1866 the* Research *lost its rudder in a wild North Atlantic storm and for two months was driven before the gale with no means of direction. After repeated and heroic efforts the ship's mate Aaron Flint Churchill was able to fix a temporary rudder and eventually they made it into Greenock, Scotland in February of 1867.*

victory over George S. Brown, an ardent anti-confederate. Thomas Killam passed away in December of 1868, and his sons Thomas Jr., Frank and John H. reorganized the family business under the name Killam Brothers; it operated as such until it was closed by Robert B. Killam in 1991, the sixth generation in the business.

More than a century has passed since Yarmouth's days of sail. In this new millennium, the only sails in the harbour now belong to yachts. The roads over which the stage-coaches once bumped are now paved, and automobiles travel at speeds unheard of a century ago. The storied Grand Hotel still dominates Main Street, but it bears little resemblance to the hotel that first opened its doors in 1894. Canada's Governor General Lord Aberdeen and his consort were guests there in 1895, and over the years, politicians, wealthy sport fishermen seeking the elusive tuna off Wedgeport, athletes and business leaders have graced its premises. Perhaps the most remarkable person to be associated with the hotel was a former employee. George Washington Kinney began working at the Grand as a bellhop when he was thirteen. At 91 years of age, he was chairman of the hotel's board of directors, capping off a continuous association of 78 years. During his tenure, which spanned much of the twentieth century, the hotel was modernized and its services expanded.

There are other reminders around town that illuminate and preserve the past. The Yarmouth County Museum is a treasure trove of records and memorabilia. The Firefighters' Museum is the only one of its kind in Canada. The Sweeney Museum, the Killam building and wharf and other local museums still portray the rich

Gold watch presented to Aaron Churchill for extraordinary bravery on board the Research.

history of Yarmouth's town and county. Near Darling's Lake, Aaron Churchill's elegant old summer home is now the Churchill Mansion Country Inn. Along the residential streets, stately old homes built by sailors and shipowners still stand. Many have cupolas, or widow's walks, where family members once watched for sailing ships in the harbour.

Sailing vessels became less popular for several reasons. The steamships were not at the mercy of the wind and they could carry larger cargos, pay lower insurance premiums and charge lower freight rates. Steamers also attracted the best young seamen, who preferred not to have to go aloft to fight frozen canvas sails or steer from an open deck while crossing the wintry North Atlantic.

The proliferation of railways across the North American continent provided faster and more reliable means of transportation compared with sailing around Cape Horn. In 1869, the opening of the Suez Canal provided a shorter route to the Orient—a route all but prohibitive to the wooden square-rigger. The industry may have contributed to its own demise: the building of wooden vessels and the export of timber and lumber products depleted the once bountiful forests, resulting in scarcer and more expensive raw materials.

Yarmouth's sailing vessels gradually vanished; shipyards became derelict, many vessels were lost and many went under foreign flags. Today, the once proud fleets live only in memory and in memorabilia, and few are the men and women who can claim they went to sea under commercial sail.

Chapter Five

THE TROOPS OF SAINT JOHN

December 1, 1872: The barque *James W. Elwell* out of Wales and bound for Valparaiso with coal has already passed bleak Cape Horn when smoke begins to pour from the ventilators. The coal in the cargo holds is on fire. Preparations are made to abandon ship but Captain John Wren decides to sail the vessel to land, where it can be beached and the fire extinguished. However, five days later, flames again burst through the hatches; the *Elwell* is doomed.

The captain orders all thirteen crew, including the stewardess, Sarah Farrington, into a lifeboat with whatever food they can quickly gather. For four days the crowded lifeboat sails through cold, stormy seas before reaching land. The occupants remain in this desolate area near the entrance to the Strait of Magellan for several days before trying to sail into the open sea in the hopes of finding a passing vessel. They are driven back repeatedly by the heavy seas and gale force wind.

Provisions are running low, and then the last of the soggy biscuits are gone. Everyone subsists on mussels and a few plants. They are suffering from exposure and exhaustion, and some are on the verge of death while others become crazed and have to be tied to the boat. Soon the only person fit to help the captain is Sarah Farrington.

The survivors, ever shrinking in numbers as more perish, still try to reach the open sea, but with no success. It rains almost continually and the nights are bitterly cold. Then the day comes when only one seaman, the stewardess and Captain Wren are left. Hope is all but gone when the White Star liner *Tropic* comes into view. The three are taken on board and restored to good health after their seventy-two-day shipwreck ordeal. Such was the hand fate sometimes dealt to those who set out to sea.

The *James W. Elwell* was part of the Troop fleet of Saint John, one of the largest family-owned fleets in the nineteenth-century Maritime provinces. The founder of the fleet, Jacob Valentine Troop, was born in Upper Granville, Nova Scotia, in 1808. As a young man he engaged in a trading business, but when he saw opportunity beckoning he moved to Saint John, where, in 1840, he opened a general provisioning store on North Market Wharf. Within a few years he was involved in a flourishing trade with the West Indies and, with his partner, Henry Pitts, he commissioned Abram Young to construct a vessel for the trade. The result was the 117-ton brigantine *Emily*, the first of at least 105 vessels that were part of the Troop fleet over the next six decades.

Trading between ports in the Maritime provinces and the West Indies truly came into its own with the arrival of the Loyalists in the

A panoramic view of the dense urban communities of Saint John and Portland in 1842. In the foreground, beyond the well-dressed excursion party, a timber raft floats past vessels on the stocks while beyond, clusters of masts crowd under the spires of the town.

1770s and 1780s. Among these settlers were shipbuilders and men who were experienced in conducting trade with the West Indies.

In 1785, when Saint John was still finding its feet, the city merchants exported more than one million shingles, nearly half a million feet of boards, 30,000 lathes, 85,500 barrel staves, over 125 masts and spars and many other types of wood products. In return, the vessels brought back sugar, molasses and 98,000 gallons of rum. By 1793, New Brunswick had built 93 square-rigged vessels and 71 sloops and schooners, many of them for employment in the West Indies trade.

Numerous other Maritime ports sent vessels south, including Halifax, Nova Scotia, and St. Andrews, New Brunswick, but Lunenburg deserves a special mention. By 1818, seven Lunenburg vessels were engaged in trade, which they continued through the nineteenth century; by the 1890s some twenty-five vessels were sailing this route and engaged in the trade. Many Prince Edward Island schooners, brigs and brigantines were sold to Newfoundland buyers who employed them in trading voyages to the islands.

By 1841 Saint John had a population of 19,000. It was a city dominated by wealthy

Howard Troop, shown here in a formal portrait with his family, embodied the prosperity that the shipping business brought to Saint John.

merchants in both wholesale and retail businesses, and in shipbuilding and all its allied trades, including timber operations, as well as in banks and insurance companies. The business elite promoted and financed a suspension bridge over the Reversing Falls, a city water supply and gaslights for the streets. This group was at least as powerful as the politicians.

Regular communication links were established with other centres in the region; three stage lines were operating between Saint John and Fredericton, each advertising a complete daily one-way passage. One line left Saint John for Fredericton every Monday, Wednesday and Friday and returned on Tuesday, Thursday and Saturday. Another stage left Saint John every Tuesday for Amherst, Nova Scotia, with stops in Norton, Sussex Vale and Dorchester. It returned to the port city on Friday. Mail service across the Bay of Fundy was provided by the schooner *Dart*, which sailed from Saint John for Digby every Saturday and returned on the following Tuesday.

The demand for ships was just beginning when Troop began building a fleet of his own. He acquired two more vessels in the 1840s and another eleven in the 1850s. On January 3, 1852, the *Saint John Morning*

News reported, "On this date there are upwards of sixteen vessels on the stocks of Saint John and neighbourhood, the smallest of these is about 300 tons, the largest 1200 tons. The demand for ships next year is said to be greater than has ever yet been known to our builders."

There were contributing factors in this demand for ships, not the least of which was the readily available raw materials and a large labour force. Wars—the Crimean and the American Civil War—created a need for ships in the 1850s and 1860s respectively, and international trade had recovered from the depression of the 1840s. Over the years there were upwards of forty shipbuilders operating in the city, ranging from early names such as Haws and Olive to the last major builders such as David Lynch and Edward McGuiggan. Then, in nearby communities, there were shipbuilders such as John S. Parker in Tynemouth Creek, J. and R. McLeod in Black River, William P. Flewelling in Clifton, Benjamin Appleby in Hampton, and James H. Moran in St. Martins. Approximately 5000 men and boys were employed directly in shipbuilding and allied trades in Saint John. Wages were low: one local shipyard paid its workers less than six dollars per week. But prices were also low. A dozen eggs cost ten to twelve cents, potatoes about seventy cents a bushel and beef about three cents per pound if bought by the carcass or half carcass.

By 1874, Saint John could claim fourth place among ports in the British Empire in terms of tonnage registered in the port. During that year, 808 vessels representing nearly 264,000 tons were registered in Saint John.

The rich, eclectic interior of Dunlop House reflects the cosmopolitan affluence that shipping and trade afforded the city in the nineteenth century.

Throughout their careers, Jacob Troop and his son Howard demanded well-built, fully equipped vessels. They came to rely on builders such as Abram Young in Granville, Nova Scotia, as well as some of the aforementioned craftsmen in the Saint John area. They also took great care in selecting competent master mariners, such as Jacob Fritz, Raymond S. Parker and W.R. Farnsworth. While builders frequently took out shares in vessels they built for the Troops,

Seasoned clerks work diligently at their paperwork in the offices of Troop & Son, the centre of a shipping empire that operated dozens of ships over a period of fifty years.

Reed Castle, Mount Pleasant residence of Robert Reed, principal of the mercantile and shipowning firm of J. & R. Reed. Built in 1854, the building was a colossal combination of Palladian symmetry and Victorian gimcrackery. Reed ultimately found the house too monumental for his tastes, and after some years moved to a modest cottage nearby.

the company also rewarded the masters with shares in the vessels they commanded.

For instance, when the *James W. Elwell* was launched on December 8, 1870, the Troops owned forty shares, the builder—Stephen King—held eight shares, as did Captain John Wren. The remaining eight shares were purchased by local investors.

When the West Indies trade waned, Troop and Son began to order larger vessels, mostly for their own fleet. Unlike many other shipbuilders in the Maritimes, Troop was not interested in constructing and selling ships. Instead, he was building on his early experiences as a merchant. Of the thirty-three vessels built for the Troops in the 1860s, only four were sold within the first two years of their launch. In the following decade, they retained ownership of all twenty-six vessels they acquired.

These deep-water vessels rarely entered ports in Eastern Canada unless there was a cargo offering of forest products. In fact, it was not uncommon for vessels, once launched, never to return to their native province.

The dashing figure of Saint John shipowner Robert Reed.

Among the first of these larger vessels were the ships *Bessie Parker* at 669 tons, launched in 1864, the *Kate Troop* at 748 tons, launched in 1865, and the barque *Annie Troop* at 511 tons, built in 1866.

In these busy years launchings usually received scant press attention. After all, there were often two launchings per week in the city. This exception appeared in a Saint John newspaper on April 21, 1880: "A good opportunity will be afforded to persons desirous of witnessing the launch of a vessel today. It has been sometime since there was a vessel launched from Portland that compares in size, finish and general appearance with that of the fine barque *Nellie G. Troop*, built by David Lynch, Portland. She is substantially constructed and, judging from her appearance, will doubtless prove a fast sailer."

Unfortunately the *Nellie G. Troop* was wrecked on the coast of Holland in the same year it was launched. If launchings normally attracted little press attention, the loss of many vessels received no more. This laconic announcement appeared in a Saint John newspaper in the spring of 1877: "*Sunny Region*, 675, from St. Thomas for Saint John, wrecked in Little Spoon Island, Maine, March 20, 1877. Built at Tynemouth, N.B. in 1868. Owned by Troop and Son. Crew saved." The announcement failed to mention that the vessel went ashore in a driving snowstorm in heavy seas, and several of the crew nearly perished before they reached shore. Another early casualty was the brig *Chieftain*, built in Nova Scotia for Jacob Troop in 1854. It foundered in 1857 with the loss of all on board while sailing from Saint John toward Jamaica. Over the years, the Troop fleet suffered extensive losses and by the time of Jacob's death these totalled 2 steamers, 14 ships, 20 barques, 5 barquentines and 5 schooners. At least six of these vessels either disappeared or foundered with all on board.

The opportunity to work for wages, both in shipyards and in manufacturing, brought many people to Saint John in its first 100 years. The 1871 census revealed a population of 41,325 persons, and also claims that there were 58 ship brokers and owners, 10 small boatbuilders, 13 shipbuilders, 9 block and pumpmakers, 8 sailmakers and 5 riggers.

Many types of businesses wanted to be as close as possible to the harbour, so like many towns and cities of this area, there were hundreds of wooden buildings built closely together along the waterfront. Sawmills and lumber yards were cheek-by-jowl with warehouses packed with canvas, oil, pitch and lumber products. And as the city had grown from the waterfront up, there was residential housing in amongst the commercial buildings. Streets were narrow, dusty in summer, quagmires in the spring and filled with snow in the winter.

Fires were inevitable. In 1837, 115 houses were lost and in 1841, when a fire began in Owen and Duncan's shipyard in Portland, more than fifty homes were consumed and 1100 people left homeless. The entire shipyard was lost, including a new vessel ready to be launched.

The Great Fire of 1877 tore through the closely-built wooden city of Saint John, destroying 1600 buildings, killing 18 people, and leaving 13,000 homeless. In this view from the Portland side of the Saint John River, the artists have crowded the Suspension Bridge with panicked citizens fleeing the conflagration.

A rakish portrait of the barque Kate Troop *at sea. The Troop fleet suffered terrible losses in the 1880s and 1890s, losing 46 vessels at sea and falling prey to a sustained financial depression.*

In 1849, fire swept down King Street into the heart of the city. But the most memorable and devastating was the Great Fire of 1877. On June 20, a conflagration raged for nine hours and left the centre of Saint John in ashes, causing some eighteen deaths, destroying 1600 buildings and leaving thousands of residents homeless. Firefighting equipment was utterly inadequate to battle such a conflagration. Funds from local businessmen, insurance payments and loans all aided in the rebuilding process. Brick and stone structures replaced wooden buildings, streets were widened and fire regulations strengthened. A brighter, cleaner city arose from the blackened ruins.

By the time this happened, the demise of sailing ships for Saint John and for the Troops was beginning to look like an inevitability. During the 1870s, Troop and Son acquired twenty-six more vessels and in the 1880s, the firm still had twenty vessels built, although demand was

The most famous of all Saint John ships, the Marco Polo. *Built in 1851, it was soon bought by the renowned Black Ball Line and outfitted for the immigrant trade. In 1852, with more than 900 passengers and 60 crew on board, it made a passage from Liverpool to Melbourne in 68 days, beating the established record and outpacing the steamship* Australia *by a full week.*

Launch days were an occasion for celebration in shipbuilding communities. Here the barque Douglas Troop *is poised to slide into Saint John harbour as an honour party crowds its decks. Along the shore onlookers in their finest clothes wait attentively, excepting the boy in the right foreground who seems rapt by the glamorous novelty of photography.*

beginning to wane. In the 1890s the Troops purchased eight more vessels—the last to join their fleet.

As Jacob Troop grew old the business fell upon his son's shoulders. Fortunately Howard D. Troop possessed the same qualities of energy, initiative and foresight as his father. Jacob Valentine Troop passed away on October 2, 1881, at the age of seventy-three. On the following day the *Saint John Globe* paid him a lengthy tribute, saying, "The port, the trade, the business of Saint John owe much to such a man whose industry, skill, perseverance and enterprise not only helped it directly but stimulated others."

When Howard D. Troop took over the business, the fleet consisted of nineteen vessels. The largest, the ship *Rock Terrace* at 1769 tons, was launched by David Lynch in 1875. Some years later, in September of 1887, the *Rock Terrace* departed Point Breeze, Pennsylvania, for Japan with a cargo of case oil and lime. The voyage proceeded without incident until January 28, 1888, when it struck a coral reef. The vessel was held fast for only a few minutes, but its hull was damaged and started leaking badly; constant pumping was necessary to keep it afloat. The captain decided to sail the *Rock Terrace* to Guam in hopes of beaching it for repairs. However, when he reached the island, a strong wind was blowing offshore, making it impossible to enter the harbour. The officers and crew, exhausted by their efforts to keep the ship afloat, decided to abandon it. When last seen, the *Rock Terrace* was sailing off on its own under reduced canvas.

In the weeks ahead the unmanned *Rock Terrace* was sighted by other vessels, but as everything appeared normal it was allowed to sail on. Some five months after its abandonment the ship was discovered on the reefs off Tarawa Island with the bottom torn out of it. In that time the ship had sailed more than 840 miles on its own initiative.

Britain's Queen, *model of a fully rigged ship made in 1839 by the shipbuilding firm of William and James Lawton of Saint John. On completion, the vessel hung in the drugstore of Dr. John Smith of Dock Street in the city and was used in a parade celebrating the turning of the sod for the European & North American Railway in Saint John in 1853. This was not based on a vessel by the same name and appears to have been constructed in and for itself to advertise shipbuilding in Saint John in general and, of course, the firm in particular.*

Above: The ship Rock Terrace *under construction, 1876. Shipbuilding in Saint John was a distinctly urban industry, carried out in the heart of the city close to the homes of those who worked in the yards. The* Rock Terrace *was owned by the Troop fleet for thirteen years before being abandoned in the Pacific where it drifted, derelict, for five months before finally grounding on Tarawa in the South China Sea.*

Left: Rock Terrace, *ship model made by Albert Carty of Saint John in about 1924, as commissioned by Larry G. Pincombe, also of Saint John.*

Above: Replacing a New Brunswick-built vessel of the same name, the Howard D. Troop *was a late entry to the Troop fleet. A handsome four-masted steel-hulled barque, it was launched in Port Glasgow, Scotland in 1892. When sold to United States interests in 1912, it was the last sailing ship operated by the firm.*

Right: The Howard D. Troop *in Vancouver, after it was sold to U.S. owners.*

Above: The ship Alexander Yeats *was launched at Saint John in 1876 and was operated as a part of the local Yeats fleet for eighteen years. Considered by some to be the handsomest vessel ever built in the city, it maintained its fine lines until it ran aground on the Cornish coast near Penzance in 1896.*

Left: Nellie G. Troop *under construction.*

Market Slip in the heart of downtown Saint John at low water. The vessels resting on the bottom are small coasters, loading and unloading with help of teamsters with their low slovens.

A commercial street in Saint John, with teamsters hauling goods up from the harbour past the city's substantial wholesale firms.

Even in the sunset years of the wooden sailing vessel, Howard Troop continued to be involved. He was the majority shareholder in such late acquisitions as the barquentines *Eva Lynch* and *Hornet*, the barques *Highlands* and the second *Mary A. Troop*, the ship *Hudson* and three terns or three-masted schooners, *LaPlata*, *Helen E. Kenney* and *Sirocco*. He also invested as a minority shareholder in several others, including the barque *Douglas* and the schooners *Eric* and *Walter Miller*.

Howard Troop was credited with being the first Canadian to acquire an iron vessel when he had the ship *Troop* built in Scotland in 1884. Five years later, it was followed by the steel barque *Nellie Troop*, which was built in England, and in 1891 by another iron ship, the Josephine Troop, launched in Scotland. In 1892, the large, four-masted steel barque, the second *Howard D. Troop*, joined the Troop fleet. At 2180 tons, it was among the larger Maritime square-riggers. It was also the last of the Troop vessels.

When Howard Troop passed away in 1912 at age seventy-three, only one vessel was left to carry the Troop house flag. The red "T" on a white diamond set on a blue field was known around the world but after nearly seventy years it would fly no more. The last of the fleet, the four-masted steel barque *Howard D. Troop*, was sold to a buyer in San Francisco. In these early years of the twentieth century there

The waterfront of the industrial heart of Saint John city was congested with large commercial sailing vessels from all over the world. The sails are hoisted while in port in order to dry them; as furled wet sails will rot and become a hazard.

were still a few of the old Maritime square-riggers sailing the seas, but their days were numbered.

Frederick William Wallace, who was among the first to collect and chronicle the story of these old Maritimers, gave them this fitting epitaph:

They were fine ships, smart ships, clean, tall-sparred,
Clothed in snowy canvas to the lofty skys'l yard,
Listing to the sea wind, wake a livid broil,
Cardiff coals to Rio, or Amsterdam with oil.
Guano from the Chinchas, hides from the Plate,
Or a load of barley from the Golden Gate,
Kerosene to Shanghai, iron from the Clyde,
All around the ports of the Seven Seas wide.
Timber droghers, grain ships, purely merchant-men,
British North Americans—gone beyond our ken.

Saint John harbour looking westward from the spire of Trinity Church, 1870. The harbour is busy with deep-water ships and barques along with the many small schooners of the city's coasting trade. In the foreground the roofs of closely-packed wood-frame houses, fuel for the Great Fire of 1877.

Chapter Six

SAMUEL CUNARD— THE HALIFAX YEARS

Samuel Cunard, who made the Cunard name famous around the world, was born in a small house on Halifax's Brunswick Street on November 21, 1787. During his childhood, Halifax was alive with naval vessels, privateers and merchant ships. The provisioning of the army and navy, the sale of prize ships and trade generated by the Napoleonic War created prosperity for the town's merchants. However, unlike the Haligonians who were spending freely, the Cunards—father and son—were cautious and thrifty by nature.

Young Samuel had no need of school once he found employment in His Majesty's lumber yard. Even in his formative years he was contemplating a career in trade. When he was in his mid-twenties, he joined his father, Abraham, in a business partnership and began trading with a vessel they purchased from the prize court. Soon the firm began acting as agents for British shipping firms, developed a thriving trade with the West Indies and expanded its fleet of vessels. It

Halifax-born Samuel Cunard, whose vision and commercial genius initiated the age of transatlantic steam navigation.

was not long before the Cunards had more than three dozen vessels under their control, and their shipping and lumbering interests were reaching into many parts of Nova Scotia, New Brunswick and Prince Edward Island.

One of the early Cunard endeavours was the establishment of a packet line to convey mail between Halifax, Newfoundland, Boston and Bermuda. It was an experience that would serve Cunard well in his later involvement with a trans-Atlantic mail service.

In 1814, Samuel married Susan Duffus, the daughter of a prominent Halifax businessman. The couple had seven daughters and two sons, but Susan Cunard's life was cut tragically short. She died while she was still a young woman, a loss from which her husband never fully recovered. Contemporary reports describe the family pew in St. George's Church as being filled every Sunday by the motherless children.

A less well-known venture of the Cunards was whaling. Vessels sailing out of Halifax had been

William Eager's drawing of Halifax from Eastern Passage in 1837, on the eve of the founding of the British and North American Royal Mail Steam Packet Company. In the foreground a small colonial cutter drifts past the growing town, its waterfront dense with the masts of sailing ships. At right a portent of the future, as a small steam-ferry puffs towards the Dartmouth shore.

Built in Quebec City and engined in Montreal for owners who originally included Henry, Joseph, and Samuel Cunard, the schooner-rigged steamship Royal William *made her unprecedented steam-powered passage from Pictou, Nova Scotia to Cowes in the Isle of Wight in the late summer of 1833. The twenty-five day passage was not spectacularly fast but convinced many, including Cunard himself, that it did "not require a coal mine to carry a steamer across the Atlantic."*

engaged in the whale fishery since 1786 when the ship *Lyon* departed for England with a cargo of sperm oil, whale oil and whalebone. That same year, three other vessels sailed out of Halifax on whaling expeditions. In 1820 the Cunards petitioned the Nova Scotia Assembly, stating that their firm had sent a vessel to the northern whale fishery but that the voyage had not been successful. Now they had fitted out another vessel for a fifteen-month voyage to the South Seas fishery. The Cunard whaling vessel was built in Dartmouth, and in 1825 a joint-stock company with capital of £15,000 was formed. However, the pursuit of whales never became a major component of the Cunard business interests.

Following Abraham's death in 1824, the firm became known as S. Cunard & Company and was contracted as agents for the East India Company and the General Mining Association of Great Britain. Cunard also continued to expand his lumber and shipping interests, dispatching his brothers Joseph, Henry and John to the Miramichi region of New Brunswick to open a branch operation there with his financial backing.

In 1825, the Halifax Banking Company opened its doors; Samuel Cunard was one of eight founding partners. His colleagues included such prominent local businessmen as Enos Collins, Henry Cogswell, William Pryor and James Tobin. Five years later, Cunard was appointed to the lofty Nova Scotia Council—the Council of Twelve—thus being recognized as a man of stature, which even the old Halifax elite could not ignore. The appointment gave him the right to the title the Honourable Samuel Cunard.

In addition to his widespread business affairs, the energetic Cunard was also community minded. He became one of the first commissioners of lighthouses in Nova Scotia, served as an officer in the militia and was a fire warden in Halifax's north end. Early in his career, Cunard sensed that the future of ocean transport lay in steam, not sail. He strongly believed that any steam-propelled vessel, sturdily built and properly manned, could arrive at its destination with the same punctuality as a train could on land. With his brothers, Joseph and Henry, he tested this belief by investing heavily in the steamer *Royal William*. Launched at Cape Cove, Quebec, in 1831 for the

Cronan's Wharf in the heart of the Halifax waterfront, south of the Cunard mercantile premises.

Quebec and Halifax Steam Navigation Company, the steamer's role was to provide a service between Quebec and Halifax that would be a faster and more dependable means of communication than either sailing vessels or land transportation.

The schooner-rigged *Royal William* carried three masts and was equipped with two engines to drive two large paddle wheels on either side of the hull. In its early runs, the engines functioned perfectly and the vessel survived heavy weather that wrecked numerous other sailing vessels. Nevertheless, although this newfangled machine was attracting widespread attention, it was not making money.

One reason for this was a cholera epidemic that swept Quebec in 1832. During the epidemic, the *Royal William* was not a welcome sight in Halifax upon arrival from Quebec. In addition, the disease was keeping travellers at home in Nova Scotia. Facing bankruptcy, the Quebec and Halifax Steam Navigation Company decided to send the vessel to England in the hopes of making a quick sale.

Prior to her trans-Atlantic voyage, the *Royal William* steamed into Boston Harbour on June 17, 1833, the first steamship ever to enter an American port flying the Union Jack. Two months later, the vessel took on 300 chaldrons of coal at Pictou, Nova Scotia, and sailed for England. Off Newfoundland it ran into heavy weather that caused leakage. Then one engine quit, but still the indomitable vessel kept going. The engine was repaired, and twenty-five days after leaving Pictou the vessel steamed into Gravesend, the first ship to cross the Atlantic solely under steam. By the following year, the *Royal William* was sailing under the Spanish flag.

In the late 1830s, Halifax's population totalled just over 14,000, encompassing about 2,500 households. The census records paint a picture of a busy port city; there was no shortage of doctors, lawyers, brewers or bakers. And although shipbuilding was not a major industry as it was in Saint John, for example, there were numerous shipwrights, sail-makers, block-makers, rope-makers and chandlers.

In 1838, Joseph Howe, the proprietor of the newspaper the *Nova Scotian*, and a newly elected member of the Nova Scotia Legislature, along with Thomas Chandler Haliburton, the author of the widely acclaimed Sam Slick stories, sailed off to tour Europe. In

During the golden age of the Atlantic crossing, the Cunard name was synonymous with the glamour of the fast passenger liner.

mid-ocean they encountered the steamship *Sirius*. Howe described the meeting: "On she came in gallant style with the speed of a hunter, while we were moving with the rapidity of an ox cart loaded with marsh mud . . . . Never did we feel so forcibly the contrast between the steamer and the sailing vessel."

It was an event that sparked a vision of steamers connecting Europe to Halifax and as soon as Howe reached London he presented a proposal to the Colonial Office. Within a matter of weeks, the British Government issued a call for tenders for a packet service to carry Her Majesty's mails between Britain and Boston via Halifax. No British firm was interested in applying alone, but one Nova Scotian was willing to undertake the venture—shrewd Samuel Cunard. He was already an experienced shipowner, and from his mail service between Halifax, Newfoundland, Boston and Bermuda, he knew the ropes. He had also had favourable discussions with some of the Clyde shipbuilders, as well as with leading British businessmen such as Richard Brown of the General Mining Association.

Cunard formed a business and called it The British and North American Royal Mail Steam Packet Company. He believed so firmly in the project that he subscribed more than three times the amount offered by the next highest of the thirty-four British investors. The contract was signed in March of 1839 with several provisions, including the institution of a regular steam service between

John O'Brien's painting of the Stag, *a 209-ton barque built at La Have in 1854. It was owned successively by several Halifax businessmen until it was lost in 1863.*

The Halifax waterfront in the steamship era. Pickford and Black was a well established mercantile firm trading with the West Indies, and were shipping agents for many of the world's foremost steamship companies. The Cunard line's operations were increasingly concentrated in a very few of the world's great ports, however, and its floating palaces were a less common sight in the city's harbour.

Liverpool, Halifax and Boston, with a subsidiary service between Pictou and Quebec during the navigation season. Also four ships were to be employed, each at least 200 feet long, steam powered and able to meet the highest standards in construction and accommodations. These vessels were built on the Clyde and named *Britannia, Columbia, Caledonia* and *Acadia*. The company also purchased the steamer *Unicorn*, which had been sailing between Glasgow and Liverpool. It was to be placed on the St. Lawrence route.

Even before any of these steamers had crossed the Atlantic, Halifax was ready to celebrate. They were aware of the developments while Cunard was in England arranging his new mail service, and after he returned in late August of 1839, an elaborate picnic and dinner were staged on McNab's Island featuring a toast to the Honourable Samuel Cunard. "Our pride as a townsman—our admiration as a merchant—may every success attend his establishment of Steam Navigation across the Atlantic." Cunard had risen to the pinnacle of success.

In May of 1840 the pioneer transatlantic crossing of a Cunard steamship, the wooden-hulled *Unicorn*, was completed in fourteen days. The Halifax wharves were jammed with people waving and cheering, and some 3000 of them went on board to tour the new wonder of ocean travel. Two months later, the new Cunard "flagship" the *Britannia* steamed into Halifax, en route to Boston where it arrived, auspiciously, on July 4. Samuel Cunard distributed some 2000 invitations to a dinner to celebrate the *Britannia*'s arrival. The new service was already a success.

The successful crossings of the *Unicorn* and *Britannia* were the source of much satisfaction for Halifax citizens as they would now be the first to receive news from Britain, as well as being the distribution centre for all mail in the Maritimes and the rest of Canada.

Howe's *Nova Scotian* was ecstatic on the opening of the packet service: "The voyage (trans-Atlantic) from thirty days is now reduced to 10 or 12. Two-thirds of the distance has thus been annihilated . . . . Thousands will soon visit us in search of pleasure or business, who would never have approached our shores had it not been for the introduction of this mode and facility of communication." It went on

to say that this would change the policies of the Colonial Office and "the true motives and standing of men and parties will be accurately scanned and valued at the source of power."

The inauguration of this oceanic service linking Halifax and England had an important by-product. For years Joseph Howe had been campaigning for a good hotel in Halifax as part of his efforts toward the construction of a railway between Halifax and Windsor. This link would provide easy access to the Annapolis Valley and its beef, poultry, pork and agricultural produce; it was currently separated from Halifax by some forty or fifty miles of road that was so rough farmers came to market only in summer and early fall, and in the depths of winter when sleighing was possible. The rail line could also link travellers to steamboats sailing between ports in Minas Basin and the Bay of Fundy, and Saint John in particular. As Howe wrote in the *Nova Scotian*: "If a good hotel were provided in Halifax and a steam communication from hence to Boston or New York, there cannot be a doubt that a very large portion of that great stream of travel, flowing through the United States from south to north every summer, could be attracted into Nova Scotia, and if it were, it would increase the income from mere passengers at least four-fold."

The advent of the Cunard Steamship Service coupled with Howe's ceaseless urgings carried the day, and in 1841 the Halifax Hotel opened its doors.

In 1846, Cunard's contract relative to his trans-Atlantic packet service was up for renewal. His success had created considerable competition from other interested shipping firms, but Cunard had a couple of strong points in his favour. First, his competition was not interested in providing winter service across the stormy North Atlantic, and Cunard was more than willing to offer a year-round service. Second, Cunard offered to equip his vessels to meet the needs of transport in time of war. His contract was renewed.

Samuel Cunard's years in Halifax came to a close when the majority of his business became centred in London; he left a son to look after his Halifax office. In 1859, he was knighted by Queen Victoria and on April 28, 1865, Sir Samuel Cunard died in London at the age of seventy-eight.

Chapter Seven

LUNENBURG'S SCHOONER FLEET

The classic image of the schooner *Bluenose* seen on postage stamps, dimes and postcards, tends to conjure up a picture of a sleek schooner, blue sky and sunlit waters. There were undoubtedly beautiful days at sea during the *Bluenose*'s time, but there was also another side to fishing on the Grand Banks. For several Lunenburg fishing families, the gale of August 24, 1927, was an event that would never be forgotten. As reported in the Halifax *Herald*, more than eighty lives were lost in a terrific gale sinking four schooners of the Lunenberg fleet—*Clayton Walters*, *Joyce Smith*, *Mahala* and *Uda Corkum*.

The losses on the *Mahala* were typical: Captain Knickle and his two brothers—sons of Archibald Knickle—were lost along with a brother-in-law and a cousin. William Tanner lost three sons while another family lost a father and a son. Of the twenty who perished on the *Mahala*, fourteen came from the hamlet of Blue Rocks. The Fishermen's Memorial in Lunenburg lists the names of 128 vessels that failed to return to port over the past 200 hundred years, including 41 that vanished with the entire crew. Also inscribed are the names of more than 690 fishermen who gave their lives to the sea.

It is slightly ironic that the 1453 French Protestants who settled Lunenburg in 1753 came from regions in Germany, France and Switzerland, all located far from the sea. Indeed, a major factor in choosing Lunenburg was its suitability for agriculture; at first, the settlers turned to farming before gradually establishing an inshore fishery. By the early 1800s schooners were venturing into the waters off Labrador in their search for cod. In those early years, the fishermen used handlines and fished from the vessel's deck. By 1829, Lunenburg boasted a fleet of 2 brigs, 16 schooners and 13 shallops fishing off the coast of Labrador and around the banks off Nova Scotia.

As the years passed, there were cycles of both good and bad economic times, but the fishing industry generally continued to expand, and the vessels got larger. In the 1850s, the average vessel measured about 50 tons; by the early 1900s, they averaged 95 to 100 tons. Those schooners were built entirely of local woods: birch or oak for the skeletal components and spruce and pine for the hull and masts. They were about 100 feet long with a beam of 24 feet and a draught of about 14 feet. It is worth noting that *Bluenose* was substantially larger than most—143 feet in length, a beam of 27 feet and a net tonnage of 99 tons.

Opposite: The handsome, clipper-bowed schooners of the Lunenburg deep-water fishing fleet anchored off the town in 1898.

Bluenose in the year of its launch, 1921. Shown here off Halifax in a sharp breeze and racing rig it displays the refined, yacht-like lines characteristic of the finest Banks schooners of the era.

The schooners carried lofty rigs. The main mast rose 115 feet above deck, and the main boom extended some 15 feet over the stern. While foot-ropes were provided, it was dangerous work furling the after end of the main sail in rough weather, and many men fell overboard.

The after cabin was usually fitted with four double berths, one of which belonged to the skipper. Storage lockers beside each berth doubled as seats. A coal stove provided heat. A clock and barometer were fastened to the forward bulkhead, and a little light came in through a glass-covered hatch that served as a skylight.

The forward cabin, or fo'c'sle, was located under the deck. Two tiers of upper and lower bunks accommodated sixteen men. The galley, with the cookstove, sink and food lockers was located in the after end of the fo'c'sle. Other foodstuffs were stored in the forward hold, which was kept cold by ice that was brought on board to keep the fish fresh. There were two fish holds, one forward of the after cabin and one aft of the fo'c'sle; each was about nine feet deep.

Like other wooden sailing ships, the design of the fishing schooner evolved over many years. Shipowners would make modifications depending on their own requirements. The *Bluenose*, for example, was the work of William Roue, a marine architect who knew how to bring together all the required ingredients in hull design and sail area that made it the fastest in its class.

Schooners were designed to withstand the rigours of the North Atlantic. They also had the capacity to carry a great deal of canvas in order to bring the catch to port as quickly as possible. In spite of all of the known losses, the typical fishing schooner that was well-handled outlasted many storms in which much larger vessels were lost.

In 1914, a typical schooner ready for sea in the 95- to 100-ton range would have cost about $10,000. It would carry crews of about twenty men, consisting of the skipper, throater, header, salter, cook and fourteen fishermen who manned the seven double dories. The youngest member of the crew was a flunkey, a young lad just beginning his career.

The introduction of the dory created significant changes in how sailors caught fish. Instead of handlining from the vessel's deck, the fishermen moved away from the mother ship in small sturdy boats taking barrels of trawl: a line perhaps a mile in length with short lines, called ganglings, attached every three feet to which the hooks were attached.

Two fishermen set out in each dory. They set their baited trawls on the bottom and after several hours, the trawls were hauled back into the dory, the fish removed, hooks rebaited and the trawls set again. This method was soon improved by a technique called "underrunning the trawl," in which the fishermen placed the trawl line across the dory and one man would remove the fish while his mate rebaited the hooks and dropped them back overboard. Thus the dory moved along the trawl line like a harvester, and since most of the trawl was always in the water, more fish were caught.

While cod was the main catch, Lunenburg vessels brought in herring from along the Labrador coast, near the Magdalen Islands and off Newfoundland's west and south coasts. Mackerel grounds in the Bay of Chaleur, off Prince Edward Island and off the coast of Cape Breton were also fished; however, both herring and mackerel stocks declined sharply toward the end of the nineteenth century.

Instead of fishing year-round, as had been the custom, by the 1880s and 1890s the industry was centred around two main voyages. The first was the spring passage to the fishing banks off Nova Scotia from March through May, followed by a summer run to the Grand Banks from early June until the end of September.

The crew's income came from a "share of the catch" system. When a fishing trip was completed and the fish were sold, certain

The fine little Lunenburg schooner Uda R. Corkum *racing close-hauled in 1921. It went down off Sable Island in the notorious August Gale of 1927, with the loss of 20 men.*

Dories towed astern an offshore schooner. Once on the fishing grounds, the dories would separate and fish long trawls of hundreds of baited hooks. If wind or fog came up suddenly, dorymen could find themselves alone in an open boat on the North Atlantic, hundreds of miles from shore.

With a look of concentrated ease, legendary captain Angus Walters takes the helm of Bluenose *in an elimination race in 1921. Walters skippered* Bluenose *to enduring fame in the International Fisherman's Cup Races in the 1920s and 30s.*

costs came off the top. The captain's commission (a percentage of the value of the catch) and the cost of bait and ice, along with the cost of salting, drying and delivery, were all subtracted from the gross return. Also coming off the gross were the wages paid to the header and throater—specialists in processing the fish aboard the vessel. The rest of the income was divided equally among the owners and the crew. The owners had to pay the cost of outfitting the vessel and providing the provisions, salt and fishing equipment; the crew paid the cook's wages and the vessel's insurance before dividing the balance into equal shares.

During the 1870s, Lunenburg firms involved in the fishery included James Eisenhauer and Company, Lewis Anderson and Zwicker and Company. Then in 1877, businessman Harry W. Adams with captains Alexander Knickle and William Arenburg formed a vessel outfitting company. Ten years later, Captain Arenburg retired and the firm was reorganized under the name Adams and Knickle Ltd., which it still goes by today.

The company's buildings are landmarks in present-day Lunenburg. The two bright red structures with the name in large white letters are located in the business district close to the waterfront. One building houses the company's offices, and for years it served as a store stocked with all the goods and equipment a fisherman might need for his vessel. The second building was a warehouse where, in later years, fish were dried. The fish were placed on large racks, slid into an enclosure and dried by warm air blown in by electric fans.

Over the years, more than thirty two-masted schooners were constructed by the local Smith and Rhuland yard for Adams and Knickle, while others were built for them in shipyards along the

The auxiliary schooner Theresa E. Connor, *now maintained as an exhibit at the Fisheries Museum of the Atlantic, Lunenburg.*

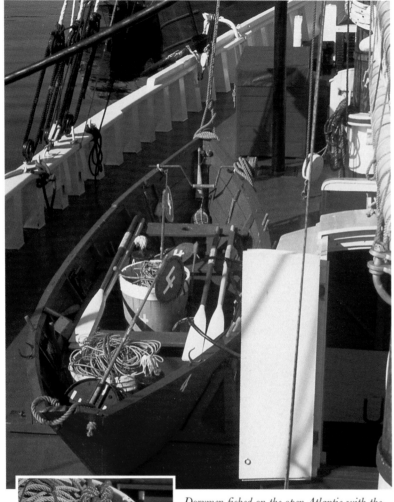

Dorymen fished on the open Atlantic with the most rudimentary gear: trawl tubs, marker buoys, oars, a boat compass, a bailer. Inset: A trawl consisted of a long stout line with lighter lines, or ganjens, spliced in every few feet, each holding a barbed cod hook.

The buildings of the Fisheries Museum of the Atlantic as seen from Lunenburg harbour. Alongside the Museum's wharves are several generations of the fishing vessels that sustained the town's economy and culture.

Opposite left:One of the chief virtues of the offshore schooner's fore-and-aft rig was that most of its sails could be handled from the decks. Topsails, however, still had to be set from aloft.

Opposite right: A menacing sea churns past the low bulwark of fishing schooner.

Above: Banks schooners owe their speed and beauty in part to the huge sail area they carry relative to the size of the hull it propels. Here a crew member in the ratlines is silhouetted against the expanse of the foresail.

The crew of the Lunenburg vessel Frank Adams *posed on the schooner's untidy decks. Seated with his arms and legs crossed is Captain "Long" Albert Himmelman, one of many fine masters to lose to Angus Walters and* Bluenose *in the fisherman's races.*

vegetables. During the whole of the same year 32,685 gallons of spirits, 6,360 gallons of molasses, 1,922 cwt. of sugar and 1,000 cwt. of coffee were imported into Lunenburg."

In wartime, some fishing vessels fulfilled other roles. For example the *McLean Clan* launched in 1920 served as a Q ship for the American Navy during the Second World War. The Q ships were armed and equipped with powerful engines then camouflaged to look like banks fishermen; they were used as decoys in anti-submarine warfare. The *McLean Clan* was badly damaged by a hurricane on its first voyage in its new role and spent the rest of the war as a training ship.

While Adams and Knickle processed other kinds of fish, cod remained its mainstay, and from the early 1900s to the Second World War, the company's specialty was salt fish. During the First World War the dried salt fish industry enjoyed its greatest growth. Norway, for example, had been offering strong competition in the Caribbean but had now turned its attention to supplying European markets. All Lunenburg exporters benefitted by this diversion.

However, by the late 1940s a shrinking demand sent the salt fish industry into decline, and Adams and Knickle began to look at other branches

south shore. The company also employed three-masted schooners to carry fish to the West Indies and return with salt from Turk's Island. West Indies trade was a familiar tradition with Lunenburgers. In the early days, residents began to develop trade with Caribbean countries. In his *History of Lunenburg County*, DesBrisay writes, "In the first three months of 1818, for example, three brigs and four schooners sailed from Lunenburg to the British West Indies loaded with lumber, wood products, fish oil, dried and pickled fish and

Salt fish from Lunenburg firms was shipped to large European markets.

Men and boys packing fish on the Lunenburg waterfront. The town sustained a thriving trade in salt fish well into the twentieth century, serving markets in Europe and the West Indies. Fish caught on the offshore banks would immediately be cut and roughly salted down at sea, then brought ashore and dried in the open air on flakes that lined the town's waterfront.

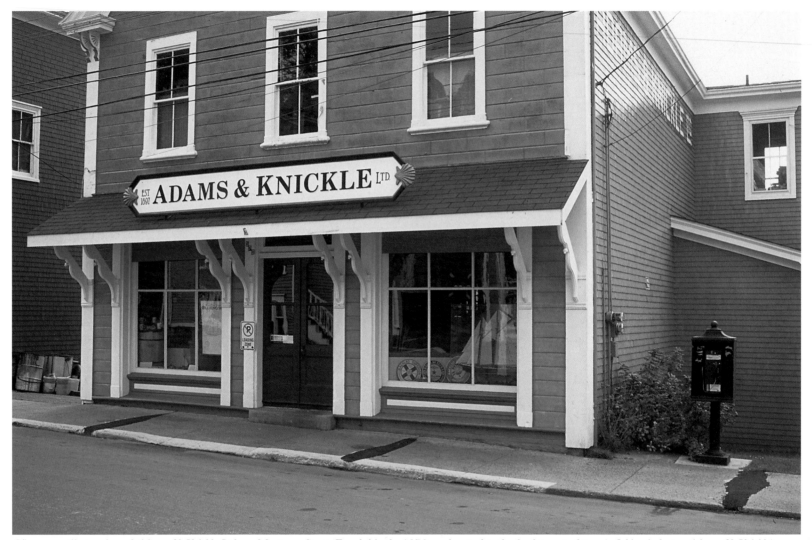

The mercantile premises of Adams & Knickle Ltd. on Montague Street. Founded in the 1870s and central to the development of town's fishing industry, Adams & Knickle's bright red establishments remain landmarks in Lunenburg to this day.

in the fishery. The partners were now the experienced veteran Harry W. Adams and Everette Knickle, son of the original co-founder. A decision was made to put the company's future in offshore scallops, and in 1954 the firm purchased Lunenburg's first offshore scalloper.

One of the last schooners employed by the company was central to the kind of tragedy that too often struck Lunenburg vessels. The schooner *Flora Alberta*, launched in 1941 as Smith and Rhuland's 187th vessel, was sailing in dense fog off Sable Island, when it collided with the freighter *Fanad Head* sailing in convoy. The schooner was cut in two, and of the twenty-four men on board only eight were rescued, and one of these succumbed soon after rescue. Among the rescued was the schooner's skipper, Captain Guy Tanner, who in 1946, 1947 and 1949 was recognized as Lunenburg's "highliner" for bringing in the largest catches in those years.

The loss of the vessel left forty-six fatherless children; all of these families faced severe hardship without breadwinners, especially in wartime Nova Scotia. The local MLA of the time, J.J. Kinley, interceded on behalf of the widows and obtained pensions for them on the basis that the sinking had been a wartime incident.

Harry W. Adams decided to have a replacement vessel built immediately. The keel was laid the following

The famous Smith & Rhuland shipyard, builders of the Bluenose. *On the stocks in this photograph is the auxiliary schooner* Theresa E. Connor, *permanently berthed at the Fisheries Museum of the Atlantic.*

A postcard of J.B. Young's shipyard in Lunenburg.

September, and on May 23, 1944, the schooner *Frances Geraldine* slipped into the waters of Lunenburg harbour. It would come to play an important role in the life of Captain Owen Creaser of Riverport, one of the last of the Lunenburg schooner captains.

Owen Creaser first went to sea in 1936 at the age of sixteen. His initial role was that of flunkey, looking after the lamps, ringing the fog bell, cleaning up after the fishermen dressed the catch, in short doing what he was told. Over the years, he became experienced in the various jobs on board fishing vessels; he also learned the skills of handling a schooner. As he worked his way up to command, Creaser sailed on such schooners as the *Marjorie and Dorothy, Haligonian,* who raced against and lost to the *Bluenose,* the *Margaret B. Tanner, Harry W.*

new American owners. In his lifetime, Captain Creaser had passed through the era of the schooner when sail was the primary means of propulsion to the power-driven schooner with its limited sailing capacity. He retired in 1975 after a fishing career spanning nearly four decades. One of his proudest accomplishments was, he says, "I never missed a scheduled trip."

Frederick William Wallace, in his autobiography *Roving Fisherman*, wrote of Captain Owen Creaser and the men of his kind when he penned the words: "He (the captain) had to be a sailor and pilot and vessel handler and command the respect and cooperation of his crew. He must be a sound judge of weather, knowing his barometer and the signs of change indicated by the wind and sky and he must know the run and set of the tides and currents. The nature of the bottoms and the grounds which fish frequent at certain seasons of the year is essential knowledge if he is to make good catches . . . . No timid, nervous, hesitating type of man would ever make good as a fishing skipper."

Fishing schooners at anchor in Lunenburg harbour as seen from the busy Smith & Rhuland yard, about 1905.

When it comes to building schooners, Smith and Rhuland are among the best in North America. Since the business began in 1900, more than 270 vessels were launched from their yard, including the *Bluenose* and *Bluenose II*. Other builders in Lunenburg County and along Nova Scotia's south shore also produced fine schooners, including John Bruno Young, who had a reputation as a shrewd businessman possessed of the highest integrity—a man whose word was as good as his bond.

Adams and the *C.A. Anderson*, where he served as mate.

While still in his twenties, Owen Creaser earned his master's ticket. Affiliated with Adams and Knickle, he was skipper of the schooners *Robert J. Knickle* and *Delawana II*, and for twenty years master of the *Frances Geraldine*, of which he was part owner. His last passage on the *Frances Geraldine* was to take it to southern waters to its

March 26, 1921. The shapely hull of the Bluenose, *festooned with flags and pennants and with masts not yet stepped, readies to take to the water for the first time. The size of the crowd attending testifies to hopes that would not be disappointed.*

The tired-looking auxiliary schooner Harry W. Adams, *low in the water at a Lunenburg wharf. As the twentieth century proceeded, lofty Banks schooners were replaced by diesel-powered auxiliaries, steel-hulled side trawlers, and factory freezer vessels. Lunenburgers have proven remarkably able to adapt to changing technological demands in the fisheries.*

Born in 1857, Young began his business career with J.D. Eisenhauer and Company. In the 1890s, he acquired water rites on a site between Duke and King streets, and established his shipyard and wharf there. Subsequently, he erected a building on the corner of Montague and King streets, which housed his office and store and which still stands to this day.

Young's shipbuilding career lasted from 1905 until his death in 1919, although he did not produce vessels during the First World War. In a decade of building his output included the two-masted schooners *Hiawatha*, *Advocate*, *Independence*, *Muriel M. Young* and the *J.B. Young*. The *Independence*, with skipper "Long" Albert Himmelman—one of Lunenburg's finest masters—was one of the many vessels that lost races to the Bluenose.

Young also constructed several three-masted schooners, or terns. One, the *Mary D. Young* launched in 1912, was the last of its type to be engaged in the fishery. Two others, the *Lila E.D. Young*, named for his daughter, and the *E.D. Bailey* were later abandoned at sea.

Walters' marine blacksmith shop, a Lunenburg institution that continued to produce custom ironwork for the town's fisheries industry into the 1990s.

Poor economic conditions in the fishery, coupled with the United States enforcing complete prohibition between 1920 and 1933, gave birth to a special export trade—rum-running. During these years, Canadian producers could export liquor, but not to nations practising prohibition. This brought the French islands of St. Pierre and Miquelon into play as a go-between.

Lunenburg vessel owners were quick to recognize an opportunity. Some fishing schooners were put to work while local builders started turning out high-powered vessels with low silhouettes. Loaded with thousands of cases of liquor on St. Pierre and Miquelon, these boats transported their illicit cargo to rendezvous off the U.S. coast, off-

Allan Morash House, built in 1888 by cousins John and Joseph Morash, is a prime example of the unique Victorian architecture that has led to Lunenburg being declared a UNESCO World Heritage Site.

cargos came to commonly mean "genuine." In 1933, the repeal of prohibition brought an end to this colourful chapter in Lunenburg's marine history.

Over the years, the fishery underwent many changes. Fishing methods went from handlining cod from the schooner's deck, to sending out dories with long trawl lines, to the huge nets of the present day. Fishing vessels began as pure sailing crafts before advancing to schooners with auxiliary engines, powered schooners with auxiliary sails and steel power-driven trawlers and draggers. Companies such as Adams and Knickle survived over the years because they learned to adapt to the changes in the availability of fish and to varying markets and market demands. They also had the resources and foresight to acquire vessels to meet these conditions.

There are still fishing vessels sailing out of Lunenburg today but of the hundreds of schooners that made up the great Lunenburg fleet only one remains, the *Theresa E. Connor*, which is permanently on display at the Fisheries Museum of the Atlantic on the town's waterfront. And of the thousands of men who operated those schooners, there are but a handful who can still be found around the waterfront remembering old times.

The Fisheries Museum of the Atlantic has been a fixture of the Lunenburg waterfront since 1977.

loading onto small, fast boats for delivery to isolated shore destinations.

The business produced an interesting paradox. While the trade was illegal, the men who operated the rum-running vessels were, for the most part, law-abiding fishermen who seized an opportunity to make some money in the hard Depression years. For example, Lunenburg's Hugh Corkum was a rum-runner who later served for many years as the town's chief of police. Another Lunenburger, Bill McCoy, developed a reputation for the quality of the rum he delivered. Unlike others, he did not water down the liquor he transported; thus the sobriquet "The Real McCoy" applied to his

Lunenburg's waterfront attracts thousands of visitors during the summer months. The museum wharf and nearby restaurants are situated in the midst of a working port, not as busy as it was one hundred years ago, but still the main commercial focus of the town.

Chapter 8

REPLICAS

The Hector

For many people in mid-eighteenth-century Scotland, living conditions were appalling. They lived in sod huts and, burdened by high rents, could barely afford to feed themselves. "An Inquiry into Late Mercantile Distresses in Scotland" written on December 5, 1772, was moved to note: "When they find their labour cannot obtain their support, after paying the rents of the land, their conclusion is made in two words, Leave It and go to that country where we believe there is Ground for us all."

These struggling people were attracted by advertisements promising them their own farmland, a year's supply of provisions and free passage to the colonies on the far side of the Atlantic.

The vessel they embarked on, the *Hector*, was 85 feet in length with a beam of 22 feet and a depth of hold less than 12 feet. It had already been employed bringing emigrants to America and was badly in need of repairs. In addition it was far too small for the crowd that was going to be jammed into its hold.

The published passenger list totals 187 men, women and children but some researchers place that figure higher. One passenger was a piper who played his way on board without a penny; such was their love of music, the other passengers offered

The Hector *framing up on the Pictou waterfront. Historical ship reconstructions offer the rare opportunity to learn about history by living it.*

to share their meagre rations with him.

The conditions below decks were abominable. Berths were simple pine boards with just two feet between them. There was no ventilation except when the hatches were open and the atmosphere reeked of bilge water, tar. brine and urine. The toilets were a few wooden buckets placed here and there. Passengers were instructed, "Don't throw the contents to windward."

The *Hector* was already weeks behind schedule when it finally departed Loch Broom in Scotland about the first of July 1773. It had not been adequately provisioned for the numbers on board and rationing had to be instituted early in the voyage. Even so the food—mostly mouldy oatcakes—was nearly gone before they reached their destination. Naturally, such conditions harboured disease: smallpox and dysentery may have caused the death of eighteen passengers, mostly children, whose bodies were delivered to the deep.

When the *Hector* was off Newfoundland a severe storm drove it back toward the British Isles; it took two weeks to recover the lost distance. Captain John Speirs wrote in his journal:

The Hector *one year after its launch in September 2000.*

Thank God the storm has passed. According to my sightings before the clouds moved in tonight, I calculate we are close to making up the lost distance. I will admit my private fears that we were in real peril during the storm . . . . This is an old vessel and in sore need of repair.

As the vessel slowly lumbered west, the captain began to express concern about the people on board:

I am afraid we should have set sail earlier than July. If early winter comes these people are going to be caught unprepared, without proper shelter.

On September 15, the *Hector* arrived in Pictou harbour after

The Hector *quay on the Pictou waterfront during the construction of the ship. The building on the left houses the interpretive centre of the Ship Hector Foundation.*

eleven weeks at sea. Its passengers disembarked at Brown's Point, just west of the present causeway leading into Pictou from Truro. They stared in dismay; instead of the cleared farmland they had been promised, all they could see was endless forest, trees up to 200 feet in height that stood so close together they shut out all sunlight. There was, however, a small clearing at Brown's Point that consisted of a few log buildings including a store, which belonged to American settlers who had arrived there in 1767.

Many of the dispirited arrivals soon left for Truro, Londonderry and other more settled areas, including Highland Village. The seventy or so who stayed erected crude shelters near the Brown's Point clearing and prepared for a harsh winter. In order to procure food, the men had to walk to Truro, some eighty miles away, through the trackless forest and deep snow. Once they arrived, they traded their labour for a bushel of potatoes and perhaps a little flour, returning with whatever they could carry on their backs.

In his 1877 *History of The County of Pictou*, Reverend George Patterson wrote:

One old woman living in 1831, used to tell that for three months their food was principally shellfish and boiled beech leaves. One calamity she described as having tried them severely. They had brought with them iron pots, but not knowing the severity of the frost, had left water in them, by the freezing of which they had cracked. Believing that they could not obtain others nearer than Scotland, she said that the loss was next to the loss of a child.

Out of necessity, these indomitable people stayed and established a community that in two generations was a keystone in the development of modern-day Nova Scotia. Pictou County politicians, scientists, educators and entrepreneurs, most of whom had Scottish origins, played significant roles in the public domain.

To honour the hardy settlers and to remember their steadfastness in the face of such suffering while crossing the Atlantic Ocean, the Pictou Waterfront Development Corporation first proposed construction of a replica of the *Hector* in 1989. The Ship Hector Foundation launched a decade-long program that included an interpretive centre illustrating the conditions aboard ship, as well as the Scotland they left and the "New Scotland" that was their adopted home. Demonstrations of shipbuilding skills and trades have been an ongoing sight at the Hector Quay. Once rigged and outfitted the replica was launched in September 2000.

The *Bounty* and *Bluenose II*

In a career spanning three-quarters of a century, the Smith and Rhuland yard in Lunenburg, Nova Scotia, launched some 270 vessels, including replicas such as the *Rose*, *Bounty* and *Bluenose II*. The building of replicas began in 1951 when a director at Hollywood's Universal Pictures commissioned the Lunenburg shipbuilder to refit two schooners for the film *The World in his Arms*, starring Gregory Peck and Ann Blyth. When the sane director was asked to work on the remake of *Mutiny on the Bounty*, starring Marlon Brando, he saw that Smith and Rhuland were contracted to build the replica of the *Bounty*. Launched in 1960 the *Bounty* cost the firm considerably more money than specified in the contract due to underestimating the labour costs. It was a loss Smith and Rhuland cheerfully accepted because of the advertising and additional commissions it created.

Bluenose has become a ubiquitous Maritime icon, a powerful symbol of the region's seafaring heritage.

After *Mutiny on the Bounty* was filmed in Tahiti, the *Bounty* sailed the oceans of the world, played a role in the film *Yellowbeard*, which was produced in Mexico in 1982, and was present at Fort Louisbourg's 250th anniversary celebrations in 1995.

Recent years have not been kind to the *Bounty*. Today it sits rotting at a dock in Fall River, Massachusetts, leaking badly, its top gear rusted away. There is a movement afoot in Nova Scotia by some who sailed on it in years past to raise the necessary funds to bring it

When Hollywood sought to recreate an eighteenth-century British warship for the 1961 film "Mutiny on the Bounty," the shipwrights of Lunenburg County were among the last in the world with the skills to build it.

home for repairs. Time will tell.

Perhaps the most widely recognized boat in Canada is the *Bluenose*, whose profile is clearly visible on the Canadian dime. The construction of an exact replica of this schooner, using William Roue's original plans, was funded by the Oland family and launched at Smith and Rhuland's on July 24, 1963. It was sold to the Province of Nova Scotia in 1971 for $1. *Bluenose II* does not race like its predecessor; instead, it travels the world as an 'ambadassor' for Canada and Nova Scotia. The crew live aboard the ship for its six-month season, learning traditional sailing skills. During the summer *Bluenose II* is often seen at Historic Properties in downtown Halifax, taking visitors on tours of the harbour. At the Tall Ships 2000, it led the parade of sail out of the harbour.

HMS *Rose*

The idea of building a replica of the British naval vessel HMS *Rose* began with John Miller, a young historian from Boston. While forming a company to raise funds for the project, he visited the *Bounty* and was impressed by its workmanship. As a result, the builders of the *Bounty*, Smith and Rhuland of Lunenbrug, Nova Scotia, were commissioned to

Bluenose II *moored along the revitalized Halifax waterfront. Nova Scotia's sailing ambassador has offered people the world over an experience of the province's shipbuilding and seafaring legacies.*

The former Smith and Rhuland shipyard in Lunenburg continues the great shipbuilding tradition that found glorious expression in both Bluenose *and* Bluenose II.

however, was so successful that town's economy was almost ruined. A bill was sent to the Continental Congress requesting armed vessels to take care of the British frigate. It can be argued that this English vessel was single-handedly responsible for the birth of the United States navy!

In April 1769, HMS *Rose* was on patrol off the American coast when it encountered the brig *Pitt Packett*. While attempting to impress the brig's sailors, the *Rose*'s first officer was killed. The seamen on the Pitt Packett were charged and a young lawyer, John Adams, was appointed to defend them. His success in obtaining an acquittal paved Adams' path to becoming the second president of the United States, an office he held from 1797 to 1801.

HMS *Rose*'s career came to an end in 1779 when it received orders to be sunk across the mouth of the harbour at Savannah, Georgia, in order to prevent French naval forces from getting close enough to bombard the British occupying the city.

Today the new twentieth-century *Rose* measures 179 feet in length, with a beam of 32 feet and a sail area of 13,000 square feet. Launched in Lunenburg in 1970, it cost roughly $325,000 to build,

construct the replica of HMS *Rose*. To ensure accuracy, the replica was built from the plans of the original ship, which were located in the Greenwich Maritime Museum in England.

HMS *Rose*'s history encapsulates the rough romanticism of the early days of the Royal Navy when impressment was sometimes the only way to keep a full company of sailors especially after a battle. Launched in Hull, England in 1757, it was classed as a twenty-four gun frigate. During the Seven Years War it saw action in the English Channel and took part in numerous attacks on French coastal positions. In 1761 it was dispatched to the West Indies and was involved in the capture of Havana and Martinique.

In 1764, following a refit in England, HMS *Rose* was sent to patrol off Newport, Rhode Island. At this time, Newport was the centre of a burgeoning smuggling business that the British navy was trying hard to eliminate, at the cost of several vessels. The *Rose*,

*Three magnificent ship reconstructions (from left to right)—*Bluenose II, Avon Spirit *and* Rose—*together in Halifax harbour, July 2000.*

The Rose, *replica of an eighteenth-century British warship, launched in Lunenburg in 1970. Like many historic ship reconstructions, the* Rose *offers sail training courses to the public, keeping maritime skills alive.*

about one-third of the quotes received from competing shipyards.

The replica's first years were spent as a dockside attraction in Newport, Rhode Island. However, by the late 1970s it had fallen into disrepair and, in 1984, HMS *Rose* was sold and towed to Bridgeport, Connecticut. There the HMS Rose Foundation was established to raise funds to repair the frigate and to finance its operation. A crew of veteran shipwrights assisted by hundreds of volunteers carried out the repairs. The finances were provided by contributions from the State of Connecticut, the city of Bridgeport and area corporations, as well as from many, many individuals.

On July 4, 1986 the *Rose* was certified as a Sailing School Vessel and declared ready for sea. Since then it has sailed hundreds of thousands of miles along the east and west coasts of the United States, to Canada's Maritime Provinces, the Great Lakes, the West Indies and across the Atlantic to the British Isles, Europe and Africa. During that time thousands of men and women have learned a little about handling a vessel and a lot about coping with life at sea under sail.

HMS *Rose* was part of the fleet of Tall Ships that visited Halifax in July 2000.

The *Avon Spirit*

When Fred Green and his stepson, Boyd Gibson, launched the schooner *F.B.G.* at Kingsport, Nova Scotia, in 1929 they probably did not know, nor care, that it would be the last commercial sailing vessel built around the Minas Basin

The small thirty-four-ton schooner lived through the Great Depression and the Second World War transporting freight wherever a cargo could be found. Its hold carried coal from Joggins, apples and potatoes from the Annapolis Valley and lumber from mills up and down the Bay of Fundy. As far as history can tell, the *F.B.G.* never left the Bay of Fundy.

During the post-war years, trucks began to transport the goods once carried by coastal vessels, and the *F.B.G.* spent more time on the beach in Kingsport, where it met its end in September 1954 during

On board the Avon Spirit, *looking aft.*

Hurricane Edna. When the Avon River Heritage Society was formed forty years later, in 1994, one of their aims was to perpetuate the story of shipbuilding along the Avon River, as well as gather a body of knowledge about the New England Planters who arrived in Newport Landing (now Avondale) in 1760. To do so, a museum was constructed on the site of earlier shipyards.

In order to help tell the story of shipbuilding the society planned to erect a skeleton of a wooden vessel and invite visitors to help build it, by fastening a plank or doing some caulking while learning about the shipwrights' skills.

This plan soon developed into the more complex project of building a replica, and the *F.B.G.*, as the last of the commercial sailing vessels, was chosen as the model. A large building was needed and a separate administrative structure formed. The replica of the *F.B.G.*, now named the *Avon Spirit*, was built in the boat shed by Snyders of Dayspring, Nova Scotia. Its keel was laid on July 13, 1996, and the launching took place on July 20, 1997, before a crowd of 4000. At 55 feet in length, its deck measured 9 feet less than the *F.B.G.*

It is a sign of the times that the cost of the *F.B.G.* could be measured in the hundreds of dollars compared to the cost of its replica, which ran into hundreds of thousands of dollars.

Following a period of outfitting and sea trials the *Avon Spirit* spent the summer of 1999 as a tour vessel at Mahone Bay, Nova Scotia. In addition, it was used in a movie filmed at Louisbourg, Cape Breton. It spent the 2000 summer season as a tour vessel in Halifax Harbour and joined some of the Tall Ships 2000 vessels in the Eastern Odyssey, visiting Charlottetown, Pictou and ports in Cape Breton.

The building of the *Avon Spirit* offered hundreds of people the chance to witness the construction of a genuine wooden sailing vessel and to recapture something of the glory of the Age of Sail.

The original *Hector*, *Rose*, *Bounty*, *Bluenose* and *F.B.G.* are long gone but each in its own way carved such a niche in marine history that their replicas ensure they will never be forgotten. First and foremost, the replicas themselves are a tribute to the traditions and skills of shipbuilding.

The Avon Spirit *at the boatyard in Avondale with the rigger putting in the final touches before launching, in 1997.*

Index